Paul Hattaway, a native 1
for most of his life. He is a
of *The Heavenly Man: The* ....
Brother Yun; *An Asian Harvest: An Autobiography*; *Operation China: Introducing All the Peoples of China*; and many other books. He and his wife, Joy, are the founders of Asia Harvest (www.asiaharvest.org) which supports hundreds of indigenous missionaries and provides millions of Bibles to spiritually hungry Christians throughout Asia.

Also by Paul Hattaway:

The Heavenly Man

An Asian Harvest

Operation China

China's Book of Martyrs

The China Chronicles 1: Shandong

The China Chronicles 2: Guizhou

The China Chronicles 3: Zhejiang

The China Chronicles 4: Tibet

The China Chronicles 5: Henan

The China Chronicles 6: Xinjiang

The China Chronicles 7: Shaanxi

HAINAN

Pearl of the South China Sea

Paul Hattaway

First published in 2023 by Piquant Editions in the UK
Also published in 2023 by Asia Harvest, **www.asiaharvest.org**

Piquant Editions
www.piquanteditions.com

ISBNs
978-1-80329-013-3 Print
978-1-80329-014-0 Mobi

British Library Cataloguing-in-Publication Data
A catalogue record of this book is available in the UK from the British Library.

ISBN 978-1-80329-013-3
Cover and Book Design: projectluz.com

HAINAN

—•—

海南

"South of the Sea"

Map of China showing Hainan

Pronounced:	Hai-nahn	
Old Spelling:	Hainan	
Population:	7,559,035 (2000)	
	8,671,485 (2010)	
	10,081,232 (2020)	
Area:	13,700 sq. miles (35,400 sq. km)	
Population Density:	714 people per sq. mile (276 per sq. km)	
Highest Elevation:	Mt. Wuzhi – 6,040 feet (1,840 meters)	
Capital City:	Haikou	1,517,410
Other Cities:	Sanya	453,819
(2010, most recent	Danzhou	418,834
census with specific	Wanning	341,654
city data)	Qionghai	302,774
Administrative	Prefectures	4
Divisions:	Counties	207
	Towns	218

			Percent
Major Ethnic Groups:	Han Chinese	6,245,329	82.6
(2000, most recent	Li	1,172,181	15.5
census with specific	Miao	61,264	0.8
ethnic data)	Zhuang	50,507	0.7
	Hui	8,372	0.1
	Yao	6,984	0.1

Contents

Contents

Foreword

Over many years and generations, the followers of Jesus in China have set their hearts to be the witnesses of Christ to the nation. Many have paid a great price for their ministry, and the brutal persecutions they have endured for the faith have often been unimaginable.

The Bible commands all believers to go "into all the world and preach the gospel to all creation" (Mark 16:15). Many foreign missionaries responded to this command in the past, traveling to China to proclaim the Word of God. They blessed the land with their message of new life in Christ and suffered greatly when the darkness clashed with God's light. Their faithful service despite great hardship was a beautiful example for Chinese believers to emulate as they served God.

China today still urgently needs more servants and laborers to take the gospel throughout the land. God is looking for people who will stand up and declare, "Lord, here am I. Please send me!"

The day of our Lord is near. May your hearts be encouraged by the testimonies of what the Lord Jesus Christ has done in China, to the praise of His glorious Name!

May the Lord raise up more testimonies that would glorify His Name in our generation, the next generation, and forever more!

Lord, You are the victorious King. Blessed are those who follow You to the end!

A humble servant of Christ,
*Moses Xie (1918–2011)**

---

* The late Moses Xie wrote this Foreword for The China Chronicles prior to his death in 2011. He was a highly respected Chinese house church leader who spent 23 years of his life in prison for the Name of Jesus Christ.

Reactions to The China Chronicles Books from Christians in China

The book you have in your hands is part of The China Chronicles, which the author is primarily writing to bless and encourage the persecuted church in China. Each book in the series is being translated into Chinese, and thousands of copies are being distributed free of charge throughout China's house church networks.

The Communist authorities in China have blocked the publication of most Christian books, especially those that deal with revival and persecution. Consequently, these books have been like living water to the thirsty Chinese believers who eagerly desire to read about the mighty acts God has performed in their nation. Here are just a few reactions from house church Christians:

We never had a good understanding of how the Lord established His kingdom in our midst, but thanks to these precious books, now we know how God has achieved great and amazing works through His servants in each province. We continue to pray that more life-giving books will flow to us!

Brother Yang, Chongqing

We believe the revival fires of the Holy Spirit will again be lit in our generation, and the mighty power of the Lord will sweep millions of our countrymen and women into the family of God. These are really amazing books. Please send more!

Brother Jiang, Hubei Province

It is very important for the children of God to understand the history of the church in different parts of China. After all, history is His Story. These are precious books, offering us in-depth accounts of the history of the body of Christ. We eagerly await each book in the series, as they will give us a more comprehensive understanding of God's glorious work in China.

Brother Zhai, Beijing

My husband and I read your book together, and we shared many thoughts and tears as we discovered testimonies we had never heard before. Our spiritual lives have been deeply enriched and encouraged. We hope to receive new books in the series as soon as they are available.

Sister Xu, Shanghai

We live in Wuhan and read your book while our city was going through its unprecedented trial. As we read how the Lord established and empowered His church, we realized that He has been in control in the past, the present, and He will continue to be in control in the future. Thank you for sharing these priceless nuggets of gold with us!

Brother Cai, Hubei Province

I shared your book with my fellow brothers and sisters in our Bible study group. We all loved it. Such living and relevant Christian history is nowhere to be found in our country, and we treasure it. We beg you to send more of these books.

Brother Zhou, Zhejiang Province

I gave your book to my son, who is a college student. He studies history, but said that none of the textbooks in his school teach anything like this. It's eye-opening and refreshing to our souls.

Sister Ping, Jiangxi Province

As the sovereignty of our Lord Jesus Christ was revealed to us through all the incidents in history, we grew acutely aware that He is in complete control, and we have nothing to fear. As a result, we now have more confidence and faith in Him, knowing that He cares for us, and the Spirit of God is at work behind the scenes, weaving together a beautiful narrative as His salvation spreads throughout our nation.

Brother Gong, Sichuan Province

The China Chronicles Overview

Many people are aware of the extraordinary explosion of Christianity throughout China in recent decades, with the church now numbering in excess of one hundred million members. Few, however, know how this miracle has occurred. The China Chronicles is an ambitious project to document the advance of Christianity in each province of China from the time the gospel was first introduced to the present day.

The genesis for this project was a meeting I attended in the year 2000 in which leaders of the Chinese house church movements expressed the need for their members to understand how God established His kingdom throughout China. As a result, it is planned that these books will be translated into Chinese and distributed widely among both the church in China and overseas. Millions of Chinese Christians know little of their spiritual heritage, and my prayer is that multitudes would be strengthened, edified, and challenged by these books to carry the torch of the Holy Spirit to their generation.

My intention is not to present readers with a dry list of names and dates, but to bring to life the marvelous stories of how God has caused His kingdom to take root and flourish in the world's most populated country. I consider it a great honor to write these books, especially as I have been entrusted, through hundreds of hours of interviews conducted throughout China, with many precious testimonies that have previously never been shared in public.

Another reason for compiling The China Chronicles is to have a record of God's mighty acts in China. As a new believer in the 1980s, I recall reading many reports from the Soviet Union of how Christian men and women were being brutally persecuted, yet the kingdom of God was growing rapidly with many people meeting Jesus Christ. By the time the Soviet empire collapsed in the early 1990s, no one had systematically recorded the glorious deeds of the Holy Spirit during the Communist era. Tragically, the body of Christ has largely forgotten the miracles God performed in those decades behind the Iron Curtain, and we are the poorer for it. Consequently, I am determined to preserve a record of God's work in China so that future generations of believers can learn about the wonderful events that have transformed tens of millions of lives there.

In the back of each volume will appear a detailed statistical analysis estimating the number of Christians living within each province of China. This is the first comprehensive survey of the number of believers in China—in every one of its more than 2,800 cities, districts, and counties—in nearly a century. Such a huge undertaking would be impossible without the cooperation and assistance of numerous organizations and individuals.

I appreciate mission organizations such as the International Mission Board, Overseas Missionary Fellowship, Revival Chinese Ministries International, and many others who graciously allowed me to access their archives, libraries, photographs, collections, and personal records. I am indebted to the many believers whose generosity exemplified Jesus' command: "*Freely you have received; freely give*" (Matt. 10:8b).

Many Chinese believers, too numerous to list, have lovingly assisted in this endeavor. For example, I fondly recall the elderly house church evangelist Elder Fu, who required two young men to assist him up the stairs to my hotel room because he was eager to be interviewed for this series. Although he had spent many years in prison for the gospel, this saint desperately wanted to testify of God's great works so that believers around the world could be inspired and encouraged to live a more consecrated life.

Finally, it would be remiss not to thank the Lord Jesus Christ. As you read these books, my prayer is that He will emerge from the pages not merely as a historical figure, but as Someone ever present, longing to seek and to save the lost by displaying His power and transformative grace.

Today, the church in China is one of the strongest in the world, both spiritually and numerically. Yet little more than a century ago, China was considered one of the most difficult mission fields. The great Welsh missionary Griffith John once wrote,

> The good news is moving but very slowly. The people are as hard as steel. They are eaten up both soul and body by the world, and do not seem to feel that there can be reality in anything beyond sense. To them our doctrine is foolishness, our talk jargon. We discuss and beat them in argument. We reason them into silence and shame; but the whole effort falls upon them like showers upon a sandy desert.[1]

How things have changed! When it is all said and done, no person in China will be able to take credit for the amazing revival that has occurred. It will be clear that this great accomplishment is the handiwork of none other than the Lord Jesus Christ. We will stand in awe and declare:

> The LORD has done this,
>   and it is marvelous in our eyes.
> The LORD has done it this very day;
>   let us rejoice and be glad. (Ps. 118:23–24)

Paul Hattaway

Publisher's Note: In The China Chronicles, we have avoided specific information such as individuals' names or details that could directly lead to the identification of house church workers. The exception to this rule is when a leader has already become so well-known around the world that there is little point concealing that person's identity in these books. This same principle applies to the use of photographs.

Several different systems for writing the sounds of Chinese characters in English have been used over the years, the main ones being the Wade-Giles system, introduced in 1912, and Pinyin, literally "spelling sounds" which has been the accepted form in China since 1979. In The China Chronicles, all names of people and places are given in their Pinyin form. This means that the places formerly spelled Chung-king, Shantung, and Tientsin are now respectively Chongqing, Shandong, and Tianjin; Mao Tse-tung becomes Mao Zedong, and so on. The only times we have retained the old spelling of names is when they are part of the title of a published book or article listed in the notes or bibliography.

The term "Evangelical" has various meanings to different people, and in some parts of the world in recent decades has come to define those with a political agenda. In The China Chronicles, the term "Evangelical" is used to describe all Christians in China who are not Catholic or Orthodox Christians.

Introduction

This photograph of a Li woman—taken by missionary Nathaniel Bercovitz—was part of a 1938 National Geographic article which brought awareness of Hainan to millions of people around the world

"The gateway to hell"

Hainan, meaning "South of the Sea," is China's largest island (not counting Taiwan). It is home to more than ten million people, distributed throughout 14 urban cities and districts, 10 rural counties, and 218 townships.

The Chinese name of the island reflects its location south of the narrow Qiongzhou Strait, which separates it from mainland China, just 12 miles (20 km) away. To the north of the Strait, the Leizhou Peninsula in Guangdong Province is colloquially known

1

as Haibei ("North of the Sea"). Explorers in the seventeenth and eighteenth centuries referred to the island as "Aynam," which is how Hainan is still pronounced in the local Hainanese dialect.

According to local legend, which may be founded in fact, "Hainan was once connected to the peninsula of Leizhou, but a volcanic disturbance caused the sinking of the stretch of land where the Hainan Straits now are."[1] For centuries, sailors have been confused by the peculiar ebb and flow of tides in the strait, and due to the danger they prefer to drop anchor in the open sea about five miles from Haikou, from where passengers board local vessels to take them to shore.

Located at the southern tip of China, Hainan is warm and humid most of the year, with tropical rainfall creating a verdant landscape. Between May and October each year the island is lashed with severe typhoons, which has caused the loss of thousands of lives over the centuries. Along the coastline, quicksand is prevalent and numerous people have perished in the deadly traps.

The interior parts of Hainan also present danger to visitors. Bubbling sulphur springs are found in various parts of the island, which instantly boil people who lose their footing while walking near them.

Visitors to Hainan often find the island deceptively large, probably because it appears on maps of China as little more than a tiny teardrop at the bottom of a huge landmass. Officially, Hainan contains more than 200 islands scattered over three archipelagos, although most people are only aware of the main island.

With a population of just over ten million people, Hainan covers an area of 13,700 sq. miles (35,400 sq. km), making it larger than the US state of Hawaii, and it contains six times as many people as the "Aloha State." By another measure, Hainan is almost as large as Switzerland, and has a slightly higher population than the landlocked European country.

Historically, Hainan was viewed as a miserable, dangerous backwater of the Chinese Empire. Rumors circulated that the "tribal savages" dwelling in the hinterland had tails, and that they frequently captured and ate their Chinese neighbors.

Although China first established a military garrison on Hainan in 110 BC, it was abandoned in 46 BC when the Han emperor decided it was too costly to keep the troops on the island. For centuries Hainan was largely forgotten, and when a disgraced official named Li Deyu was exiled to Hainan during the Tang Dynasty (618–907) he unflatteringly described the island as "the gateway to hell."

In a 1938 *National Geographic* article—which brought Hainan to the knowledge of much of the English-speaking world for the first time—the author noted, "The Chinese sometimes term their far southern possession 'the Tail of the Dragon.' The name is quite appropriate, too, for to the bulk of Chinese people Hainan is far more remote and mysterious than even Mongolia, Turkestan [Xinjiang], or Tibet."[2]

"Isle of Palms"

As the twentieth century unfolded, a nicer nickname for Hainan was coined. "The gateway to hell" was consigned to history and "Isle of Palms" became a more convivial description of the tropical paradise.

Half of Hainan sits on volcanic ash just below the topsoil, which creates a good environment for agriculture. A Presbyterian missionary in the early twentieth century described some of the many kinds of mouth-watering tropical fruit in Hainan, including "papayas, breadfruit and jackfruit, litchis, mangoes, coconuts, custard apples, bananas, guavas, pineapples, figs, several varieties of berries, and several citrus fruits. Among

A palm tree on the beach at Tianya Haijiao ("end of the earth") in southern Hainan
Hilke Maunder

the latter are limes, pumeloes, and a variety of green oranges even more delicious than grapefruit."[3]

Much of the eastern part of the island is covered with wetlands, while many rivers flow out of the central mountains to different points around the province. Today, over 60 percent of Hainan remains covered with lush forests.

Being a tropical paradise, Hainan is home to a great number of animal, bird, and plant species, with more than 570 different animals and 4,600 native plants found on the island. Until the twentieth century, the forests of Hainan were home to man-eating tigers, but they were captured or hunted to extinction, and today few large animals remain in the wild. A 1930s article highlighted some of the wildlife that was prevalent on the island at the time:

Hainan's wildlife includes two species of deer—the muntjac, and a large deer five feet high at the shoulder called the "mountain horse." There are porcupines, foxes, flying squirrels, monkeys, and pythons which are captured alive using iron hooks and transported to the Chinese border where the Hainanese eat the flesh as an aphrodisiac; there are also boars, a small species of leopard, black gibbons, and numerous birds such as parrots, pheasants, mynas, pigeons, and doves.[4]

Ethnic complexity

The Li people are acknowledged as the original inhabitants of Hainan, having arrived from the mainland at least 2,000 to 2,500 years ago. Their language is related to other Tai varieties, indicating the Li were originally part of the ancient Yue race that gave birth to today's ethnic minority groups in south China such as the Zhuang, Dong, Shui, Bouyei, and Dai.

Li children from different tribes in the mountains of Hainan
Imagebroker

For centuries the Li dwelled on the island without competition from other races. It was not until the tenth century that many Cantonese and Hakka peasants arrived in Hainan, seeking arable land to establish new communities. They encountered the Li people, who at the time lived on the plains, and violent conflict resulted, with the Li being pushed off their land into the rugged mountains of the interior, where they remain to the present day. During the Song and Yuan dynasties (960–1368), the Li people staged 18 large-scale uprisings against Chinese rule. After the government subdued the Li and established control, waves of Han entered Hainan, especially from neighboring Guangdong and Guangxi provinces. Before long the Han became the dominant ethnicity on the island.

Eight of every ten people living in Hainan today are Han Chinese, belonging to a complex myriad of linguistic groups, due to waves of migration to the island over many centuries. The largest group of Han in Hainan are known as the Hainanese. Their ancestors arrived by boat from Fujian Province in east China about 600 years ago, from areas where most people speak the distinctive Min Nan variety of Chinese.

The seafaring history of the Hainanese extended to other countries. In the nineteenth and twentieth centuries, many Hainan men traveled across the South China Sea and found work in Malaysia, Thailand, Vietnam, and Myanmar, often as servants, miners, or laborers on rubber plantations. Many left their families in Hainan and took second wives abroad, traveling back and forth each year. Some of the early Hainan missionaries were surprised to meet men who could speak fluent English from their time spent in Southeast Asia.

A modern Babel

Today the Hainanese, with their unique language, continue to dominate the Han population in Hainan, but significant enclaves of Mandarin, Cantonese, and Hakka-speaking Chinese also inhabit the coastal areas of the island, while the town of Xincun on the southeast coast is inhabited almost completely by Dan Chinese, who are traditionally known as the boat people of south China. Most of the Dan are employed in the fishing and pearl cultivation industries.

Early Evangelicals who arrived in Hainan with the ability to speak Chinese found the local vernacular almost incomprehensible. In 1900, Presbyterian missionary William Leverett visited a community of Chinese who claimed to speak Mandarin, and said they were the descendants of the poet Su Dongpo and his followers, who were exiled to the island in 1097. Leverett lamented that the thousand-year separation from mainland China had rendered the language "woefully departed from its pristine beauty."[5] Still today, Mandarin speakers from the mainland often find themselves baffled when trying to converse in the national language with people in rural parts of Hainan.

Leverett, who was based in the town of Nada in central Hainan, said the small district "surely deserves to be called a modern Babel, for within a radius of 30 miles there are at least eight different dialects or languages spoken. In this district there are, also, differences in the character of the people, differences in customs, and often differences in dress."[6]

The second largest Chinese group in Hainan are the 670,000 Lingao people, who inhabit many counties on the north side of the island in and around the city of Lingao (formerly Limko). Although the government has been quick to place the Lingao under the Han nationality, historical records considered them Li people. While many Lingao today are bilingual in other Chinese vernaculars, their heart language is part of the Tai family.

Western Hainan also contains some interesting ethnic groups, including 95,000 Cun people, who are officially classified as part of the Han nationality even though their language is like one of the five Li tribal languages in Hainan. Not far away, 1,000 Fuma people—who inhabit a single village—are considered a distinct ethnicity by other people in the region. The government has also classified the Fuma as part of the Han nationality even though they, too, speak a Li language.

The officially-recognized Li and Miao minority groups are concentrated in the mountainous inland areas of the province, while more than 30,000 people from Vietnam and Indonesia have been repatriated to Hainan since the 1950s. Most of the Vietnamese and Indonesians—many of whom are Christians—were settled at the Xinglong Overseas Chinese Farm in eastern Hainan, where many are engaged in rubber and coffee production.

Hainan is also home to more than 50,000 Zhuang and 7,000 Yao people, while the most distinctive of Hainan's peoples are the more than 8,000 Utsat Muslims who live near the city of Sanya. Speaking a language from the Malayo-Polynesian family, the Utsat are believed to be related to the Cham of Vietnam and other peoples in Southeast Asia. Since the mid-1980s, Islamic scholars from Malaysia have visited the Utsat, teaching them the Qur'an and solidifying them in the Islamic faith.

Little is known about the origins of the Utsat, although one report in the 1940s said, "More than 200 years ago on the southern tip of the Island of Hainan a ship load of Muslims was shipwrecked. These people remained and not far from the harbor built a village in which they are still to be found. Recently they have rebuilt their mosque."[7]

In 2020, after a severe crackdown in northwest China sent more than two million Muslims into concentration camps (which the Communist Party cynically calls "vocational training centers"), the Utsat people were also targeted despite living thousands of miles away in Hainan. The Utsat were instructed by the community not to wear traditional Islamic clothing and head coverings, and signs in Arabic as well as Muslim architecture were also banned, in keeping with President Xi Jinping's crackdown on all expressions of non-Han culture and religion.[8]

Hainan in the twentieth century

The Japanese invaded Hainan in February 1939 and ruled the island during the Second World War, resisting all efforts to repel them. After the United States ended the war in 1945 by dropping two atomic bombs on Hiroshima and Nagasaki, Japan withdrew from Hainan, having gained nothing from six years of senseless violence.

Despite their long history of conflict against Chinese rule of the island, the Li joined forces with the Communists during the

The Japanese invasion of Hainan in 1939

war against Japan. As a result, the mountainous center of Hainan was designated an autonomous area, with four counties today being Li autonomous counties, while in two other counties the Li have shared autonomy with the Miao (Kim Mun) minority group.

The Guomindang (Nationalists) resumed control of Hainan after the Japanese surrender, and a struggle with the Communists ensued. Hainan did not fully come under Communist control until May 1, 1950, seven months after Mao Zedong had officially established the People's Republic of China in faraway Beijing.

The last days of the Guomindang hold on Hainan were terrible after it became apparent that they were not able to hold out against the resurgent Red army. When large numbers of Communist troops crossed the strait and entered Hainan, the Guomindang tried to relocate all 70,000 of their soldiers to Taiwan, but they were too late. At least 33,000 Guomindang were slaughtered by the advancing Communists, with many troops watching helplessly from the decks of their transport ships as their friends were mowed down on the dock by People's Liberation Army machine guns.

After China began to open its doors to the outside world under the leadership of Deng Xiaoping in the 1980s, Hainan was quickly identified as a place with much potential to attract foreign investment.

A big boost for Hainan's development came when the island was granted status as a province in 1988. Before that, since 1950, Hainan had officially been part of Guangdong Province. When it became a separate province, Hainan was also declared a "Special Economic Zone," which helped it attract investment and develop its tourist industry.

Corruption on a grand scale

Billions of dollars were pumped into Hainan during the 1980s, leading to one of China's most famous corruption cases. Beijing allocated $1.5 billion to modernize transportation on the island. Instead, local officials under the leadership of Lei Yu used the money to buy 90,000 new cars and trucks from Hong Kong at discount prices, of which a number were sold on the Chinese mainland for huge profits. The officials also purchased 2.9 million television sets, 252,000 video recorders, and 122,000 new motorcycles.[9]

Beijing's response to the massive corruption was to block Hainan from receiving any more foreign currency allocations for ten years, and Lei Yu's actions so infuriated the government that there was talk of the island having its status as a province revoked.

The upside to the corruption was that for years, visitors to Hainan enjoyed more modern transportation than almost anywhere else in China. Tourists could travel from one end of the island to the other in just a few hours, aboard comfortable, air-conditioned minibuses.

Hainan came into worldwide attention in March 2001, when an American spy-plane collided with a Chinese air force jet and was forced to make an emergency landing on the island. The incident, which cost the life of the Chinese pilot, led to a tense standoff as the Chinese detained 24 American navy personnel for 11 days. The relationship between China and the United States was greatly strained for a time.

Rebranding Hainan

From the start of the new millennium, the authorities in Hainan accelerated plans to enhance the island's profile by turning it into a popular resort destination. With Hainan located at roughly the same latitude as Hawaii, hundreds of seaside hotels and guesthouses were constructed. Airports were built or upgraded and before long, planes carrying sun-lovers and adventurers from Europe, Japan, Australia, and other parts of the globe were landing in Hainan.

In addition to being pitched as a glamorous resort destination, the Hainan government secured the rights to host international golf and tennis tournaments. Hollywood celebrities were flown to Hainan in a bid to promote the island to millions of people around the world who otherwise would have never heard of it.

The authorities also did a good job selling Hainan as a desirable tourist destination to the booming Chinese middle class, resulting in an influx of millions of domestic visitors each year.

To accommodate the growth, Hainan Airlines—which started as a small provincial company with a few planes—has grown to become the fourth largest airline in China, connecting to 500 destinations throughout Asia.

Food trucks for tourists on the beach at Sanya
Natalia Garidueva

The influx of billions of dollars into Hainan created a bubble in the housing market, with prices for apartments comparable to what people pay in many Western countries. To cool down the market, in 2018 the government introduced new rules, with non-residents required to pay a deposit of at least 70 percent of the price of property. To further curb speculators, owners are not allowed to sell their property for at least five years. The changes appear to have had little lasting effect, however. While many Hainan residents—who recently lived in poverty—now find themselves millionaires, others have been left behind and can no longer afford to live on the island.

In 1991, an American missionary and his family were the first Westerners granted permission to live in Hainan since the Communist Revolution. He was shocked when some of the recent photos of Hainan used in this book were shared with him prior to publication. In a way that visitors to Hainan today will scarcely find believable, he recalled what life on the island was like in the 1990s:

> When we arrived, the tallest building on the island was six stories. In terms of train service there was a single line from Sanya to Dongfang and it was small gauge and traveled so slowly that it took all day to make the one-way trip so there was one round trip every two days. There was one very narrow paved road around the outside of the island and one through the middle from Haikou to Sanya. It took eight hours to catch a bus from Haikou to the west coast.
>
> It was almost impossible to make an international phone call, and there were no such things as residential telephones. The postal service was horribly unreliable, so it was useless to mail anything.
>
> The airport at Haikou had no radar or other electronic services so all landings had to be visual. Planes couldn't land or take off if there was fog or if it was dark. We had a ferry to Hong Kong, but unfortunately it sank around 1993.

Only four percent of the population had gone to school beyond fourth grade, so very few people could speak Mandarin. The western two-thirds of the island was not really controlled by the government but rather by gangs and private militias. That made traveling in that area very dangerous. Even into my lifetime, some of the Li tribes practiced cannibalism.

I am sure I would be completely unable to recognize anything there now, even though I knew it like the back of my hand when I worked there.[10]

Hainan today

Although much of the economy in the interior of Hainan remains based on agriculture, with rice, rubber, pineapples, and sugarcane among its main produce, the huge push toward tourism in recent decades means that approximately 80 percent of Hainan's GDP is derived from the hospitality industry.

*Downtown Haikou in 2022. Hainan's capital has
emerged as a key financial and research hub*
Petergraphy

14

Spurred on by the Communist Party loosening restrictions that allowed citizens of 59 countries to visit Hainan for 30 days without a visa, the influx of tourists has been phenomenal, growing from 20.6 million in 2008 to over 76 million in 2018. The island has become a favorite playground for rich Russians, who before the 2022 war with Ukraine, would flock to Hainan's beaches to escape the bleak northern winters. Japanese and South Koreans are the next two most common nationalities who visit Hainan.

The avalanche of new money which poured into Hainan also brought an explosion of vice and crime, as multitudes of holiday-makers sought to add carnal pleasures to their trips. Thousands of prostitutes appeared on the island, with countless massage parlours becoming the front for procuring drugs and other illegal activities. The Hainan authorities have launched periodic crack-downs in a bid to retain Hainan's image as a family destination, but their efforts only appear to have forced the vice and crime deeper into the shadows.

The booming tourist industry in Hainan came to a screeching halt in 2020, when President Xi Jinping's fanatical "zero Covid" policy forced the entire island into lockdown for months after a small number of infections were detected. Thousands of foreign and domestic tourists, who had flown in to enjoy some sun and relaxation, were stuck on the island and forced to submit to a strict regime of testing and isolation. Those who were cleared of the virus found that other provinces in China had banned all flights from Hainan, so they could not leave. If statistics are ever released for tourist numbers in Hainan from 2020 to 2022, they will show a dramatic fall.

A major announcement was made on June 1, 2020, when the Chinese government declared all of Hainan Island now a free trade port, with a goal to transform Hainan into the largest economic zone in China. The authorities have actively reached out to multi-national companies in a bid to lure them to set up headquarters on the island. Some China experts believe President Xi is hoping Hainan will partially replace Hong Kong, where democratic principles have frustrated the Communist Party's plans in recent years, causing its economy and reputation to shrink.

Hainan is a province experiencing transformation at warp speed. Those who return to the island just several years after an earlier visit can scarcely recognize it. The once sleepy tropical island now even boasts its own space center near the city of Wanning, which China uses to launch satellites into orbit.

There were practically no roads in Hainan until the 1950s, but today a high-speed railway encircles the island, with trains travelling up to 160 mph (250 km/h). The travel time between Haikou in the north and Sanya in the south is now just 90 minutes, including several stops at stations along the way. A century ago, visitors endured up to a month of dangerous travel over steep mountains and through dense tropical forests to traverse the island.

Bracing for conflict

Although many visitors to Hainan today see a burgeoning tropical paradise, Chinese military expansionism in recent years has China watchers nervous about what many see as an inevitable war coming to the region, with only the perilous Taiwan situation more likely to be the catalyst for widespread conflict between China and the West.

More than 50 disputed islands, reefs, and tiny deserted shoals sit in the strategic South China Sea, where an estimated $5 trillion worth of trade passes through each year. These specks of land are likely to become the flashpoint for armed conflict in the not-too-distant future. The trouble began when the Chinese government decided to rewrite maps and create bogus claims to all the disputed islands and unoccupied reefs and atolls in the South China Sea. They decided the whole region belongs to them, even though the international community had long considered them part of the countries whose coastlines are much nearer. China, however, came up with unlikely stories to "prove" their historic ownership of the entire South China Sea, including the discovery of "ancient maps," supposedly proving their dubious claims.

Undeterred by a chorus of international criticism, China has aggressively expanded its influence in the area, much to the consternation of their neighbors the Philippines, Vietnam, Brunei, Malaysia, and Indonesia, all of which claim part of the territories now occupied by China. While critics derided Beijing for their laughable claims of historical ownership, China focused on the vast reservoirs of oil and other minerals believed to sit beneath the ocean floor. They pressed forward quickly and aggressively, catching their neighbors off-guard with the speed of their expansion.

In July 2016, China's plans suffered a setback when the United Nations dismissed their claims of "historic title" in the South China Sea. Beijing reacted furiously, contemptuously dismissing the ruling and warning other countries that any attempt to push the Chinese away would be met with overwhelming military force.

From their base in Hainan, China sent heavy machinery and quickly filled in the land above some of the South China Sea's atolls and reefs. They then claimed the freshly-formed islands were now permanent land masses, and the flag of the People's Republic of China was firmly planted in their newly manufactured "territories," which all fall under the administrative banner of Hainan Province. The Communist Party also quickly constructed runways on some of the reclaimed land, and fighter jets were soon landing and taking off as the sabre-rattling continued.

When the United States and other governments have complained about China's illegal annexations in international waters, China has responded by sending warships to the area to defend their "homeland." The value of these deserted rocks to Beijing can be seen by the virility of their denunciations whenever the United States or ships of other nations sail through the area.

At the same time, President Xi Jinping has cleverly developed closer relationships with the offended countries in the region, providing billions of dollars of aid and investment in return for their silence. The Philippines, especially after the colorful President Rodrigo Duterte came to power in 2016, has largely acquiesced to Chinese demands. Their complaints have gradually subsided, despite some of the disputed Spratly Islands sitting just 100 miles (162 km) from the Philippines coast, but more than ten times that distance from the Chinese coast.

And Hainan plays a major strategic role in China's global expansionist plans, with a large People's Liberation Army submarine base located near Sanya on the south coast. The base is built into caverns surrounded by steep hills, which can hide up to 20 nuclear submarines from spy satellites. The harbor, meanwhile, is large enough to accommodate aircraft carriers.

China has shown it possesses both the will and the military hardware to enforce their claims in the disputed South China Sea, while Hainan is also said to be the base from where China launches their so-called "weather balloons" that circumnavigate the globe collecting data. The balloons, one of which hovered over sensitive military sites in the United States in early 2023, are part of an "aerial surveillance program" run by the People's Liberation Army out of Hainan."[11]

Religion in Hainan

Whereas much of north and central China saw temples and idols smashed by the Red Guard during the Cultural Revolution (1966–76), communities along the South China coast have largely retained their beliefs and superstitions to the present day.

Statues of the goddesses Mazu and Guanyin are dotted all along the Hainan coast. These deities have been worshipped for centuries as protectors of fishermen. A massive statue of Guanyin, built on the southern coast in 2005, stands 354 feet (108 meters) high, making it taller than the Statue of Liberty.

A host of other gods and goddesses are revered throughout Hainan. Animism still prevails in the tribal areas, with shamans wielding powerful influence in Li villages.

Hainan's religious traditions are overlaid with ancestor worship, which keeps millions of people trapped in fear and unwilling to risk offending their ancestors by changing their beliefs. These rituals are solidified by a powerful clan system that remains in place throughout the province. Family lineages stay closely bound together, with each clan having its own set of favorite deities and protective spirits.

Christianity

Some readers may find it surprising that an entire book in this series has been devoted to Hainan—one of the smallest and least populated of China's 31 provinces and regions. Indeed, in our experience few long-term missionaries to China have ever set foot on the island, nor have many Chinese Christians from the mainland ever ventured across the narrow strait to this Pearl of the South China Sea.

As you will read in the pages of this book, a new religious force, Christianity, has taken Hainan by storm in recent decades.

Above: A huge statue of the goddess Guanyin in southern Hainan
Juha Öörni

Below: A young man worshipping at the feet of Guanyin
Song Yuan

Those who despise Christianity and see it only as a Western belief system have been left dismayed as the Living God has displayed His power and glory among the people of Hainan, primarily through an indigenous movement that swept across the island, transforming hundreds of thousands of lives from darkness to light.

Originally, it was planned that Hainan would be combined with nearby Guangxi in *The China Chronicles*, but during the research phase it quickly became apparent that despite its size, Jesus Christ has done such a wonderful work in Hainan that it warrants its own book.

Around the world, Christians love to read accounts of great revivals in history, when God supernaturally intervenes in the course of a nation, sweeping multitudes into His kingdom with awesome power and grace. For almost all readers, this book will be the first time they have heard of the Hainan Revival of the 1990s and 2000s. It has never featured in a book, even though the number of people converted in it is larger than the famous, well-documented Welsh Revival of the early twentieth century.

If you are someone who desires to read of revival, miracles, and testimonies of entire communities transformed by the gospel, you will be delighted by the accounts of the Hainan Revival. Before reaching that part of the book, however, we encourage you to attentively read the chapters which tell of the faithful witness of foreign Evangelical missionaries in Hainan over a period spanning eight decades.

As you read about the dedication of these normal men and women, be aware that the extraordinary events that transpired later were partly because those missionaries carefully laid a firm foundation for the gospel on the island.

Catholics in Hainan

Centuries of promise and persecution

Catholic missionaries have the distinction of having commenced work in Hainan a full 250 years before the first Evangelical appeared.

The first Catholic to set foot in Hainan was the Portuguese missionary Baltasar Gago (1520–1583) and two unnamed Franciscan colleagues. After serving in Japan for eight years, Gago was blown off course when the ship that was carrying him back to Europe was caught in a typhoon. After drifting to Hainan, the three men were mistaken as vagabonds, or pirates, and thrown into prison. They remained incarcerated on the island for two months before their identity as Europeans was confirmed and they were allowed to continue their journey. Gago later wrote of his harrowing experience, "I saw in the prison a large room where there were more than 100 prisoners, all of whom were nearly naked and had their feet locked in blocks."[1]

The first Chinese Catholics in Hainan came about because of the influence of the famous Italian missionary Matteo Ricci, who never visited the island but affected it from his base in faraway Beijing. Arriving in the nation's capital in 1598, Ricci adopted an approach to influence the highest levels of Chinese society in politics, academia, education, science, medicine, and other fields. Respected as a great Western scholar, he was able to share the gospel even to the inner court of the Wanli Emperor.

One of Ricci's converts in Beijing was an important emissary whose son, Paul Wong, became a follower of Christ after he relocated to Hainan. Seeing need for urgent help if the gospel was ever going to be established on the island, Wong traveled to Macao and begged the Catholic leaders to send a priest to Hainan to baptize his wife and children. Wong's request was finally honored when Pierre Marquez was sent to Hainan in March 1632, and "Paul Wong's wife, three sons, one of his slaves, and four grandchildren were baptized."[2]

As Marquez had difficulty learning the local languages in Hainan, he was recalled to Macao and replaced by Benoit de

A 1610 portrait of Matteo Ricci

Mattos, who had been serving in Fujian Province and had little difficulty learning the related Hainanese dialect.

For a time, the Jesuit missionaries enjoyed the favor of both officials and the people of Hainan. When he searched for a property to buy, Mattos was surprised to secure a well-appointed house for a fraction of the price of inferior properties. He learned later that the locals believed the house to be haunted, so nobody else dared to live there. The missionaries wasted little time on Hainan, and according to reports,

> The first year over 300 persons were baptized. In 1636 Hainan was divided into four districts.... Each had a well-fitted and adorned church building. In the year 1637 the fervency of Christianity was at its height and over 300 persons were baptized at one time, but Satan was infuriated to see himself compelled to leave his kingdom and persecution began.[3]

Alarmed by the level of interest in Christianity, the Hainan officials carefully hatched a sinister plan to destroy the new religion. Mattos was falsely accused of hiding weapons and ammunition in his home. A mob was sent to lynch the missionary, and even though no contraband was found, his protestations of innocence fell on deaf ears. Realizing the leaders of Hainan would ceaselessly persecute the local believers while he remained on the island, Mattos sailed for Macao, leaving the flock in the care of a Chinese catechist. Alas, the Bible teacher was poisoned to death in August 1640, leaving the church in Hainan without a leader.

In 1644, Mattos was able to return to Hainan, but three years later the Manchus invaded the island after they gained control of China and established the Qing Dynasty. The Manchus were shocked to find European missionaries already established at the extreme edge of their empire and Mattos—along with missionaries from Poland, Portugal, and Italy—suffered terribly. Although he survived the torturous ordeal at the hands of the

Manchus, when additional regiments were sent to subdue the island in 1651 and 1652, the faithful Benoit de Mattos was thrown into the ocean and drowned.

A series of bitter decrees against foreigners and their religions were issued during the 1660s and 1670s, but the Catholic remnant survived in Hainan, until all records of the work suddenly came to a halt.

Although details are sketchy, it appears a plague struck the island in the 1680s, decimating the population and causing the deaths of many of the Catholics and their converts. Two centuries later, in 1883, a startled Evangelical missionary found an

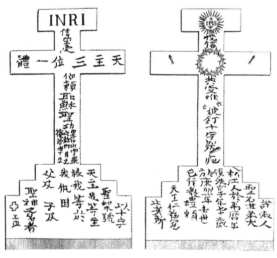

A sketch showing the front and back of a typical cross that many Chinese believers had erected above their graves in the 1600s and 1700s, including in Hainan. A translation of the Chinese text says (front of cross): "I believe, I hope in, I love God in three persons, relying on the sacred merits of Jesus Christ. I firmly believe, I ardently hope for the pardon of my sins, the resurrection of my body, and the life everlasting"; and (back of cross): "I believe that He has suffered; that He was crucified; and that He died."

old Catholic cemetery in the hills outside Haikou. He wrote of his discovery,

> Hundreds of monuments over the graves have the cross plainly cut upon them, and the names of Chinese converts have all the particulars of age, residence and position given. The inscriptions on several of the Chinese tombs as well as the size and shape of the monuments show them to have been men of high position in the church. Conspicuous among the others are the tombs of three Europeans. One of these was a German, as the Latin inscription shows, who died October 9, 1686, after being in Hainan eight years.... The other two seem to have been Portuguese who died in 1681.
>
> Many of the Chinese tombs bear nearly the same date; and the annals of the Prefecture record a plague of unusual fatality that swept over the island about that time. The existence of a cemetery, so finely located, with such numbers of tombs of respectable people, certainly indicates that at one time the Catholics had a large following in Hainan.[4]

The land containing the cemetery was seized by the Japanese during the Second World War and turned into an airfield. Today, there are no gravestones left to commemorate the deeds and commitment of those early Catholic pioneers.

After a long lapse, a second wave of Catholic work on the island was started by French missionaries in 1849. They received a rough reception, with the first priest to arrive in Hainan being beaten so severely that he died from his injuries.

Despite their long history, the Catholics struggled to gain a foothold among the population for much of their time in Hainan, partly because work on the island was administered from faraway Hong Kong and Macau. When the Vatican placed Hainan under the jurisdiction of Guangdong Province in 1908, Catholicism on the island had nearly died out, with only 300 to 400 Catholic believers living in Hainan at the time.[5]

Despite centuries of effort, few Catholics live in Hainan today. This photo of a Haikou church and its priest was taken in the late 1980s
Bridge

By 1950, Catholic work on the island had recovered, with one study finding there were 3,419 Catholics in nine parishes throughout Hainan.[6] The number of church members stagnated during the following decades of Communist rule, however, and in 1988 one source stated there were only 3,000 Catholics on the island at the time.[7]

Carl Jeremiassen

The mysterious pirate hunter

Although Catholic missionaries beat their Evangelical counterparts to Hainan by centuries, they struggled to maintain a strong presence on the island, and by the mid-nineteenth century their numbers had dwindled to a few hundred.

The first Evangelical influence among the people of Hainan appears to have been spread by the enigmatic German Karl Gützlaff, who first resided in Indonesia in 1826 before settling down in Bangkok, Thailand. While there, he encountered traders from Hainan. Gützlaff noted in 1831,

> I had an extensive intercourse with this people. They took a particular delight in perusing Christian books and conversing on the precepts of the gospel. And almost all of those, who came annually to Bangkok, took away books, as valuable presents to their friends at home. Others spoke of the good effects produced by the books and invited me to visit their country.
>
> Humbly trusting in the mercies of our God and Redeemer, He will accomplish, in His own time, the good work which has been commenced. I would invite some of my brethren to make this island the sphere of their exertions, and to bring the joyful tidings of the gospel to a people anxious to receive its precious contents.[1]

Nearly four decades passed until 1869, when an eccentric sea captain, Carl Jeremiassen, became the first known Evangelical missionary to step foot on Hainan Island. Jeremiassen is always purported to have been from Denmark, but it is more likely that he came from today's Greenland, which was controlled by Denmark at the time.[2]

He was employed by the Qing government to hunt down pirates on the high seas, which he did by commanding a small steam ship. During those years, "he had many trying experiences with typhoons, and fought and conquered in 14 sharply contested battles with smugglers and pirates."[3]

While he was in the employ of the Guangzhou Customs Service, Jeremiassen "came into contact with vital Christianity," and his life was transformed. Upon reaching Hainan, the 34-year-old Dane changed his occupation and began to preach the gospel throughout the island. By the end of his first year, he had visited numerous towns and villages throughout the island. A report of his first year in Hainan said,

> Jeremiassen at once began to study Hainanese and also opened a dispensary, where he was able to cure many of the patients who came. Before he had been here a year he made a complete circuit of the island, treating the sick and distributing Christian literature in each place he visited. During the year he made his headquarters in Haikou and went on itinerating trips through the country.[4]

Carl Jeremiassen, who was given the Chinese name Ji Wentian, was quite a sight to the locals, few of whom had ever seen a foreigner before. He was described as "a red-bearded giant." His successor, Henry McCandliss, had this to say about the enigmatic Dane:

> Although a subject of the King of Denmark, he spoke English well, and from long residence on the coast of China knew the language and ways of the Chinese. In many long journeys he dispensed, surveyed, and preached in nearly every part of Hainan. As an un-ordained minister he was not specially authorized to baptize, so he sought the aid of Presbyterian ministers from

Guangzhou.... I was the first to arrive and started to learn the language and to help him with the medical work....

It was remarkable what he could do in a market town in a stay of about four days: Iridectomies and operations for cataract, entropion, harelip, crushing of vesical calculi [bladder stones], splinting of fractures, opening of abscesses, extraction of bullets, and a surprising number of other procedures.... The number of bad teeth that could be extracted in a morning was surprising, and the fortitude of the patients, who would feel around to see if there were any other teeth that could be spared, was even more so. If I could have a dollar for every tooth pulled since I took over the medical work from Mr. Jeremiassen, I could build a nice little hospital. Often, I have thrown open the dispensary doors and said, "Those who have teeth to be pulled, come first."[5]

Unlike most other provinces of China, where the first missionaries are well-known and documented, Hainan's first Evangelical remains a man of mystery, with some later historians even questioning his existence.

Even the timeline of Jeremiassen's life and service is uncertain. Many sources state that he arrived in Hainan in 1881, but other research places him on the island 12 years earlier in 1869.[6]

No photograph remains of Jeremiassen, but what is known is that he was a larger-than-life character who came from a background completely contrary to the normal, respectable route taken by other missionaries of his era. The sea captain never attended seminary nor was he educated in the ways of refined speech and behavior.

What God did see in the redeemed Jeremiassen, however, was a man with a passion for His Word and a steely determination to share Jesus Christ with as many lost people as possible. It was said that this rough diamond of a man had been so transformed by God's grace that he changed his career from being "a seeker of criminals for punishment to a seeker of souls for salvation."[7]

A fresh approach

After a time as an independent missionary, Jeremiassen decided he needed some more advanced medical training if he was to succeed in his new career. He served a two-year apprenticeship at the Canton (Guangzhou) Hospital, and after acquiring additional medical skills he returned to Hainan in 1881 where he settled in Fucheng, near Haikou.

From his base in the north of the island, Jeremiassen conducted many "long, extensive treks into the interior, dispensing medicine and gospel truths. He traveled with a faithful servant who was dumb, and a colporteur provided by the British and Foreign Bible Society."[8]

After a time, the reformed pirate catcher gathered enough funds to purchase the Wu clan's ancestral hall in Fucheng. After cleaning and remodeling the building, he turned the main hall into a church. Later, however, he was strongly opposed by the local Chinese, so he moved to the town of Nada and established a gospel hall there. At the time, Jeremiassen was the only Evangelical missionary in Hainan.

Gradually, other parts of the body of Christ became aware of the presence of the unique Carl Jeremiassen. The *Chinese Recorder and Missionary Journal* made mention of him in this 1882 report:

> On December 7th, B. C. Henry returned from a trip through the Island of Hainan in company with C. C. Jeremiassen. They were everywhere received with great kindness by the inhabitants—both the Hainanese and the native tribes. Jeremiassen had numerous applicants for medical treatment. Books were readily bought, and hospitality was everywhere cordially extended to the travelers.[9]

The Guangzhou-based missionary mentioned in the above quote, Benjamin Henry, enjoyed his time with the Danish pioneer. He wrote a fascinating report of his trip, in which he referred to Jeremiassen only as his "friend":

> The people were eager for books and medicines which we supplied as quickly and as fully as possible. Our intention was to leave early the next day, but the people returning from the market had spread the news of our arrival and the fame of my friend's medical skill through the villages far and near, so that on the following morning our doors were besieged by an eager and impatient throng, gentry, and common people....
>
> Over 100 were treated and prescribed for, and many sent away for whom nothing could be done. The readiness with which they took the foreigner's medicine and submitted to operations was surprising. The number of villages represented shows the country to be very populous and the appearance of the people indicated a good degree of prosperity. Nearly all of them spoke Li, an interpreter being necessary when conversing with them. We received only respect, friendliness, and pressing invitations to remain among them.[10]

When the duo reached another part of Hainan, Henry remarked,

> As soon as we could get disengaged of our traveling gear I took a supply of books and drew a large part of the crowd into the street, where under a shed in the midst of pouring rain, the books were sold as fast as they could be handed out, until the principal temple, turned into a temporary dispensary, attracted the people to witness or receive the benefit of the doctor's skill.[11]

Within three years, Carl Jeremiassen's preaching produced a small group of converts in the town of Nada. As he was not an ordained minister, Jeremiassen asked the Presbyterian Mission in Guangzhou to send someone to baptize the new converts. Henry Noyes traveled to the island in 1884, and after examining 20 candidates he agreed to baptize nine of them. This small group formed the nucleus of the church in Nada. Noyes remarked,

I had a pleasant trip with Mr. Jeremiassen well into the interior of Hainan. The farthest point we reached was 90 miles [146 km] from Haikou, the treaty port. At the end of the island journey, we reached a market town where is the first Evangelical chapel ever established on the island. This chapel was opened some ten months ago. Already there is a Sabbath congregation of between 40 to 60. Twenty applied for baptism. Nine were baptized, and most of the others are hopeful inquirers.

The people are everywhere friendly. All this must be very encouraging to Jeremiassen. His arduous and persevering labors deserve to be crowned with abundant success. It is a privilege I shall not soon forget that I was permitted to share with him the pleasure of receiving into the Church of Christ the first Evangelical Christians baptized on the island of Hainan.[12]

The gospel had started to take hold in different parts of the island, with a special letter being hand-carried 130 miles (210 km) across the mountains to the missionaries in 1884, begging them to return to one inland area. Jeremiassen and two Chinese assistants had briefly visited their district a few years earlier, but the message of Jesus Christ had lodged in people's hearts and minds, and they were eager to know more. The invitation read:

We invite you, honorable gentlemen, to examine our petition. On a previous occasion, you, honorable persons, came and preached the gospel in the home of Ngou in the village of Dang-Toa. Many people gathered to hear you, and many believed.

Several gentlemen counselled together in reference to building a chapel in Dang-Toa.... If there is no chapel, how can the gospel be proclaimed? If there is no leaven, how can the meal be leavened? But if there is leaven the meal will gradually rise. If there is a chapel and the Word is preached, then gradually one man will proclaim to ten, ten to 100, a hundred to 1,000, a thousand to 10,000. Is not this like the mountain stream? One place will then be all leavened by the gospel.[13]

In 1885, Henry Noyes returned to Hainan and again visited Nada, where this time he reported,

> At Nada, where nine persons were baptized last year, there are now 50 names on the roll of inquirers. A chapel has been requested at Nanfeng, 12 miles [19 km] further inland, and in many other places the people are anxious for the missionary to come. The coast and the northern half of the island are occupied by Chinese, while the uncivilized aborigines of Malay origin occupy the southern interior. These aborigines are exceedingly friendly, treating the missionary with great consideration, and urging him to open schools in their towns.[14]

An unexpected change occurred in Jeremiassen's life in 1885, when he abandoned his life as an independent missionary and joined the Presbyterian Mission. Many thought the former sea captain would never be able to find a suitable wife, but he surprised many by marrying Jeanne Sutter from Switzerland, who was the first female missionary on the island.

Trouble erupts

With a people movement to Christ beginning to unfold in parts of Hainan, the enemies of Christ rose in strong opposition. Just two days after Jeremiassen and Noyes left the new converts in Nada, an attempt was made by local officials to extort money from the fledgling believers. Although influence from the British Consul at Haikou helped stem the persecution, the money and possessions seized from the Christians were never returned.

A Hakka rebellion broke out on the island in 1886 and 1887, and several thousand Chinese troops were dispatched to put down the insurrection. Unaware of the dangers of such hot and humid, mosquito-infested conditions, many soldiers contracted and died of malaria. Faced with a hopeless situation, the Chinese General Fang called for Jeremiassen's help. Once the missionary administered quinine to the afflicted soldiers, all of them recovered.

Fang was overjoyed and asked how he could repay the red-bearded giant. Jeremiassen suggested that a plot of land be provided with suitable buildings to take care of the sick. The general gladly agreed to this proposal, and plans were made to construct a mission compound with a medical dispensary, chapel, and a small home for Jeremiassen and his wife.

What appeared to be a wonderful gift to help advance the gospel turned out to be a millstone around Jeremiassen's neck. The general was reassigned to another area just after he promised to provide the land and buildings, and the Danish missionary was left to deal with stubborn officials who refused to honor the general's pledge. A rumor then spread throughout the community that a large church was being constructed for the missionary, and that all people would be forced to forsake their ancient ways and embrace the "foreign religion."

When the dispensary was built, the local magistrate ordered that it be destroyed within three days. Presbyterian missionary Frank Gilman, who had only just arrived on the island, was told that his wife and child would be murdered if Jeremiassen didn't agree to give back the land.

Meanwhile General Fang, who had originally made the deal, was persuaded to change his mind, and he demanded Jeremiassen return the land. The courageous missionary, who had formerly faced down treacherous pirates on the open seas, refused to bow to the general's demands.

A message was sent to the Dane, threatening that if he didn't forsake the land a proclamation would be issued telling the people to tear down the buildings. Jeremiassen replied, "The general may do as he chooses. I will not take down the building, and if it is torn down by his orders, he must remember that he is tearing down my property, for which he will be held responsible."[15]

Jeremiassen called General Fang's bluff, and he prevailed. The buildings remained.

The Hakka insurrection had brought much pain to the Christian community at Nada, and when some stolen cattle came into the possession of one of the baptized believers in 1889, the man was arrested and "on account of this he was afterwards beheaded. Because the missionaries could not interfere and save his life, the membership at Nada was reduced during the year by nearly half, through the defection of those who saw no good in belonging to a society which had so little worldly power."[16]

Independence regained

During the years that Jeremiassen functioned as an independent faith missionary, he enjoyed the freedom to go where he pleased and to roam around the island reaching people for Jesus. After joining the Presbyterian Mission, the free-spirited sea captain grew increasingly frustrated, scorning the denominational structure and resisting all attempts to control him.

Finally, by 1893 Jeremiassen was at his wits end. He resigned from the Presbyterians and organized his own independent mission. Again free to indulge his passion for open-air evangelism, Jeremiassen and his wife Jeanne traveled extensively on long trips into the Hainan mountains. Their annual report for 1894 told of one of their journeys:

> The first four months of the year were for the most part spent among the aboriginal tribes...having daily services and healing the sick.... We made Fanja our headquarters for a fortnight while we made daily visits to the numerous villages hidden away among the mountain glens, where we found the people very much interested in what we had to tell them about God and His wonderful dealings with men.[17]

From the early days of Jeremiassen's missionary career, he had been burdened with the need to provide God's Word in the languages of the people he was trying to reach. Driven by an unquenchable zeal and sense of urgency, he soon decided

> to undertake a translation of the New Testament, which was to be published in Roman script and in the Hainanese colloquial script....
>
> Although the translation of Matthew was ready by 1886, various delays prevented its publication until 1891. The Gospels according to John, Luke, and Mark followed, in that order, in the years from 1893 to 1895. In this latter work he was assisted by his colleague, Frank Gilman.
>
> In 1899 the British and Foreign Bible Society published the Acts and all the books from Galatians to Jude, except for the Epistle to the Hebrews. In the same year a Harmony of the Gospels was privately published. Work had also commenced on the Old Testament, the books of Genesis and Haggai to Malachi being published in 1901, when Jeremiassen died in the south of the island.[18]

The mystery persists

At the end of 1900, Jeremiassen took his wife and four children to the south coast of Hainan, but while there, a typhoid epidemic engulfed the area. He was taken sick with fever, but with no other foreigners to help, his family faced the daunting task of getting their delirious leader to the nearest medical facility at Haikou on the north Hainan coast. He died on the boat during the second day of the voyage. The extraordinary first Evangelical missionary to Hainan perished at the age of 54.

Carl Jeremiassen's close coworker Frank Gilman offered this touching tribute to his fallen friend, and his two decades of service for Christ among the people of Hainan:

He explored and made maps of the whole island, secured land and erected buildings, did successful medical and itinerating work, translated most of the books of the New Testament into Hainanese script and did much to prepare a Chinese literature in the same form, and was able to see most of his work brought through the press. While he was not always able to work in harmony with his colleagues, he always retained their admiration and affectionate regard….

With difficulty his body was brought to Haikou, where it was followed to the grave by the whole foreign community and by many mourning Chinese friends.

So closed the career of a brave, tender-hearted, self-denying, strong, and useful man, who, as a fighting captain, a devoted friend, husband, and father, and as an explorer, pioneer missionary, medical practitioner, and translator into an obscure language, filled his life was labors which might arouse to emulation many men in the various spheres he displayed his activity.[19]

Even Jeremiassen's death failed to curb the sensational stories about this larger-than-life character. Rumors circulated throughout the island that the red-bearded giant had been seen walking into a live volcano and had gone to be with the gods.

In reviewing Jeremiassen's ministry he was an energetic worker, but his zeal might have been better utilized by a longer-term, more in-depth approach. Among the Li minority tribesmen, who had no prior knowledge of Christianity, the seed scattered in their villages soon fell on rocky ground.

Years after Jeremiassen's death, another foreigner visited a Li village in the interior of the island, where the people told him how, long before, they had been visited by a Westerner "who stayed for only about an hour. His name they did not know, but he distributed many papers showing a strange god with a beard!"[20]

In more recent times, as Christian researchers gained a clearer understanding of the key role that Carl Jeremiassen played in establishing the gospel in Hainan, some have attempted to trace his origins, only to come up empty-handed. Frustratingly, it later emerged that the story of Jeremiassen's life was handed over to Danish explorer and author Henning Haslund-Christensen in 1923, but it appears he never published it. Although eternity will reveal the full identity and mystery behind Carl Jeremiassen, what is known is that this courageous and hard-working man was the first non-Catholic to spread the gospel in Hainan, and many lives were transformed because of his labors.

Jeremiassen spent most of his time in Hainan based at the small town of Nada, which is now considered part of Danzhou City. It is not coincidental that today Danzhou contains more than 80,000 Evangelical Christians—the highest number of believers among all the cities and counties in Hainan.

Henry McCandliss

Dr. Henry McCandliss at the age of 59

The first missionary ever sent out by the US Presbyterian Mission Board after its formation was Henry McCandliss, who arrived in Hainan in 1885. Upon arrival, he was excited by the potential he saw and declared, "The whole island is open to missionary work."

Henry, a native of Iowa, commenced his work by caring for malaria patients and leprosy victims near Haikou, the capital of Hainan. Locals could not believe a Westerner would "stoop so low" as to give his life to treat despised lepers. He established the Haikou Gospel Hospital (now renamed the People's Hospital), and in 1887 he founded the Haikou Church, just two years after his arrival on the island.

After serving three years as a single man, Henry fell in love with Olivia Kerr, the daughter of missionary-doctor John Kerr in the Chinese city of Guangzhou. They were married in 1888 and moved to Hainan. Over the years, Henry often traveled inland to Nada and other districts to follow up Carl Jeremiassen's work. Like his predecessor, McCandliss combined medical clinics with the proclamation of eternal life. He was careful to not separate the two, so that patients were left with no doubt as to the motive of the missionary and the source of the blessings they received. In one of the first mission dispatches from Hainan in February 1888, it was reported, "In Hainan, the medical mission has treated 3,000 persons within two months and has preached the gospel to them all."[1]

While McCandliss was establishing the work, anti-foreign sentiment was on the rise in Hainan, as China feared the French had ambitions to take over the island and add it to their ever-expanding colonial possessions in nearby French Indo-China (today's Vietnam, Laos, and Cambodia). In 1891, the Qing government built the Xiuying Fort in Haikou to defend the island against a possible French attack. Five large cannons can still be seen at the site.

Like many other later Hainan missionaries, Henry was stunned by the complex demographic composition of the church in Hainan. Once, while vising the town of Nada, he noted,

> Sunday congregations vary from 30 to 70.... Regular Sunday services are held in the street of the market. These are curious meetings.... Singing and a large, well-illuminated picture of some Bible subjects draw the crowd. Hakka, Mandarin, Li, Hainanese or Cantonese are used, according to the crowd that gathers.... There are 22 professing Christians there.[2]

Decades later, as he looked back on his early days in Hainan, Henry McCandliss recalled,

> I tried to get a house with an upstairs room, but the only house that seemed possible was just behind the Temple of the god of War. The man in charge asked us if we were willing to live in a haunted house. He said that a couple of years ago a new official had come to the city, bringing many followers, and 28 of them had died at that house from a pestilential fever. Since then no one had dared to live in the house, but perhaps we "foreign devils" would not mind. We took the house, used plenty of carbolic, boiling water, and smoking sulphur, and made it habitable.[3]

Trouble in Qionghai

After a while, Henry and Olivia decided to branch out and began to research ways to reach more of Hainan. They moved 68 miles (111 km) south to the town of Qionghai, where they purchased a four-acre farm, which included a dilapidated house. With the property title in hand, McCandliss went to the magistrate to have his purchase stamped, but trouble erupted, as foreigners were not legally permitted to live outside the "treaty port" city of Haikou.

The middleman who had assisted in the purchase was thrown into prison, and when Henry went to visit him, the magistrate was infuriated and threatened to beat the missionary with a stick if he ever went to the prison again. These actions were designed to make McCandliss feel unwelcome and leave Qionghai, but Henry and Olivia were not the type of Christians to bow to intimidation, and they refused to leave.

After six months, they were finally able to get the man released from custody after paying a considerable sum of money, but they knew if they left Qionghai for a moment their property would be seized, so they never left it unoccupied. When they attempted to do repairs, however, the magistrate appeared with 50 men and drove them off the land. Henry wrote, "The workmen were told that any further attempt at building would result in their being put into pig baskets and carried to the sea. We held on to the place for six years, and then the purchase money was returned."[4]

More hardship came upon the pioneers when Olivia tried to open a school for girls. Almost before the plans were announced, placards appeared all over Qionghai and neighboring towns, warning people that the foreigners wanted to kidnap girls and sell them to the flesh market in Hong Kong. From that time on, every time Olivia appeared in public she was insulted by crowds of angry people and pelted with rocks and rotten fruit.

Finally, after years of turmoil, Henry and Olivia abandoned their plans to live in Qionghai and returned to Haikou. Rumors abounded that the missionary-doctors stole the eyes of Chinese children to use in secret concoctions, so they cut a section of wall out of their surgery room and installed a wide window with metal bars, so the fearful townspeople could always see what was going on inside.

Most of the cases he treated were related to malignant malaria, and almost invariably, whenever he had to cut open a patient, McCandliss found the person's insides infested with worms, which spread rapidly in Hainan's humid tropical climate. Many adult patients died, especially those who had contracted syphilis or cholera, while the infant mortality rate at the time was at least 50 percent. Only after McCandliss had been in Hainan for 20 years did he realize that most of the infant deaths were the result of newborn girls being deliberately poisoned by their disappointed parents, who wanted a male heir.

As the years passed the work did not get easier, and Henry and Olivia seemed to live in a constant state of stress and danger. Often when a patient died, a commotion would follow with the victim's family threatening to kill the doctor unless a large sum of money was paid for compensation.

In 1900, as the Boxer Rebellion was devastating the Christian community in north China, a plague swept Hainan, and 6,000 people died out of a population of 40,000. McCandliss grew deeply discouraged at the time. The mission ran out of money, and his attempts to recruit Chinese medical workers to come to Hainan invariably failed, for the island was still considered a cursed backwater in the minds of most Chinese.

The McCandliss family served the people of Hainan for four decades, during which they oversaw the formation of churches all over the island. Many other Presbyterian missionaries joined the work, while all three of the McCandliss children went on to serve as missionaries in China.

Just before he retired to the United States in 1925, the 66-year-old Henry McCandliss wrote an article summarizing his four decades of sterling service in Hainan and how the kingdom of God had grown there. His words serve as an ideal way to finish this profile on the life of the outstanding figure in the first century of Evangelical Christianity in Hainan. The veteran missionary-doctor wrote,

> In 40 years, there have been 67 missionaries attached to the Hainan Mission. There are now 30. Eleven have been transferred to the mainland. Seventeen are retired and are now living in the United States. Nine have died—a mortality of nine in 67 is not heavy. The great difficulty in Hainan is that the warm, humid climate makes it difficult to recover from a serious illness. For this reason, we now have a year at home after every five years of service.
>
> The evils that continue to grieve us are banditry and piracy. We are never without the dreadful evidence of their work. From our house in Haikou we have often seen on the mainland 20 miles away the smoke of burning villages. What was happening under that smoke we could only conjecture by the nature of the damage suffered by those who would be brought to us a day or two afterwards.
>
> Mrs. McCandliss and I have been in the hands of bandits ourselves, and it has put us in a position to sympathize with others who encounter similar experiences. Even bandits, however, are not ungrateful. A few weeks ago one of our evangelists and eight Christians were captured, and after being stripped of valuables were taken before the bandit chief. He said to his followers, "Why are you capturing these people who took the bullet from my side?" So, he prepared a boat and sent the captured men back to Haikou.[5]

After news of his retirement reached mainland China, the *North China Daily Herald* published this tribute to the veteran missionary:

> McCandliss began work when foreigners were objects of superstitious dread and fear, and when Western medicine was considered a black art. Patiently, faithfully, skillfully, Dr. McCandliss has carried on his ministry of healing, and has seen the work grow from a tiny dispensary in Qionghai to a hospital for 150 in-patients in Haikou.
>
> The Chinese greatly regret his leaving.... In the invitations they gave to attend the farewell gathering in Haikou, which they planned in honor of the doctor, they mentioned 388,518 patients and 2,395 maternity cases as the number of those who have come under his care.[6]

After retiring from missionary service in 1925, Henry McCandliss went to his eternal reward while living in California six years later. Olivia followed him two years later in 1933. They had lived in Hainan for 40 years, laboring sacrificially for the people and giving a tremendous witness of faithfulness, integrity, and hard work. Many of the elderly Hainan pastors who later endured Communist persecution had been discipled by Henry McCandliss when they were teenagers.

1890s

A trickle of Presbyterian pioneers

After the long and faithful witness of the McCandliss family, a steady flow of other American Presbyterian missionaries came to Hainan over the years. For decades they were the only missionary society with workers on the island, but with great determination and faith, they endured innumerable hardships and succeeded in planting the seed of the gospel in the hearts of people throughout Hainan.

Teachers and students at the Presbyterian School at Nada, 1890s

Many of the new arrivals had a steep learning curve in the differences between life in Hainan compared to their homeland. In 1893, missionary-doctor James Anderson found that most patients paid him for their treatment with food or articles of clothing, as cash was of no use to them. Anderson was startled when he was told that,

> One sick man, long unable to work, had raised money for the journey by the sale of his wife to another man. Another young man, having been unable to work for some time, had been dismissed by his wife, who then married someone else. She had been honorable enough, he said, however, to give him back the $15 he had paid for her, and with this money he was able to live at the hospital while the doctor sought to effect a cure.[1]

Because of the multi-linguistic nature of the Ledong area in southwest Hainan, the Presbyterians imported a printing press to the town, which produced thousands of Gospel booklets and tracts in the colloquial Hainanese Roman script for distribution throughout the island. For years the press met the growing demand for information about Christianity, as people in Hainan desired to know more about Jesus and the Bible.

Female missionaries

Starting with Jeanne Jeremiassen, Hainan emerged as a mission field where a steady flow of female workers was determined to serve. In the nineteenth century, however, Western culture dictated that women were to stay at home, and even married women were put through a rigorous process before many mission boards considered them suitable to join their husbands in China.

Those women who did make it to Hainan invariably gravitated toward ministry to Chinese women, leading girls' schools, or taking care of orphans. Great was the fruit that these activities produced over the years.

Mission work in Hainan was dominated by the Presbyterians, who gradually relaxed their views toward female missionaries. Hudson Taylor's China Inland Mission, however, sent hundreds of laborers into other provinces of China, but few were ever assigned to Hainan. At the time, some CIM leaders held very strong views regarding female missionaries.

Many shared the opinions of a CIM leader, Dr. Arthur Douthwaite, who believed women would struggle to learn a new language, would be slow to socially adapt to a foreign culture, and that the "weaker sex," should not be exposed to the risks of living in a disease-ridden place where violent persecution could erupt at any time. In 1898, Douthwaite said,

> Women are liable to certain functional disorders, which are readily provoked by the disturbance of their emotions, in consequence of the break-up of home associations, the long voyage, the entire challenge of surroundings on reaching their destination, the effect of a strange climate, the study of a difficult language, and the enforced sedentary life while engaged in study.
>
> I don't say that all lady missionaries are thus affected, but many are, and unfortunately, functional disturbance sometimes leads to structured change, and a long list of evils follows.[2]

While CIM continued to focus on other parts of China, the number of female missionaries in Hainan steadily grew into the twentieth century. Some of the most effective laborers for Christ on the island during this missionary era were women, who accessed the grace and power of God while impacting parts of Chinese society which men had no opportunity to engage.

To counteract the reluctance of some mission societies to send women to the field, several mission statesmen focused on the size and urgency of the task of evangelizing the world before Christ's return, and they emphasized that all God-anointed workers, regardless of gender, should be mobilized and sent into the harvest fields of the world without delay. In one rousing speech, the famous preacher John Mott, who served for decades as the leader of the YMCA and the World Student Christian Federation, said,

> Consider the difficulty of acquiring the Chinese language; the dwarfing conservatism and over-running pride of China;...ancestral worship, with its terrible grip on man, woman and child; Chinese Buddhism, with its ignorant, immoral priesthood and gross forms of idolatry;...the universal ignorance which enslaves the people to a thousand superstitions;...the amount of physical suffering which is incredible and appalling, and the utter absence of medical science apart from one medical missionary to every two million people; and the 180 million women who are virtually in slavery....
>
> When we remember these things, and the dreadful fact that here is a country not regulated by the living, but by the dead, can we question that China presents the greatest combination of difficulties of any mission field?[3]

Famine at the close of the century

Toward the end of the nineteenth century, a sustained famine plagued the people of Hainan after the crops withered and entire communities faced starvation. The missionaries responded by doing all they could, and for months their focus was directed on helping people survive. In 1898, the Christian and Missionary Alliance reported,

> A terrible famine prevails in Hainan. From all points of the island the news that arrives at Haikou is heartrending. In the interior there is found on the pathways the bodies of poor wretches dead of hunger. The Chinese are buying rice in Tongking [now north Vietnam] to send to Hainan, where the natives buy it up.[4]

As the decade concluded and the dawn of a new century appeared, a new threat hung over Christian work in Hainan.

The French had expanded their empire into Southeast Asia, establishing "French Indo-China" in parts of today's Vietnam, Laos, and Cambodia; French gunboats had sailed up the river into Bangkok, Thailand, where they forced the Thai king to agree that Laos now belonged to France.

Hainan appeared likely to be the next place the French would raise their flag, and military skirmishes between French and Chinese troops had already occurred in the border region for many years. The people of Hainan were in distress, for although they were not fond of being ruled by an emperor in faraway Beijing, it was far preferable to being governed by the hated French imperialists.

In August 1898, an insurrection took place at Nada in Hainan, which many feared would provide the French an excuse to invade the island. A large group of rebels, reinforced by refugees from Guangxi, threatened to overrun Hainan. Chinese soldiers arrived and seized the Presbyterian Mission buildings in Nada, using them as headquarters to repel the rebels. A mission magazine reflected the sentiment of the time: "Should it not be suppressed, there is an opportunity for French interference. The French are using vigorous measures to protect the native Christians in nearby Zhanjiang, and are extending their influence in southern China, which at present is very disturbed."[5]

In the end, France never did invade Hainan, with their expansion stopping at today's border between Vietnam and the Guangxi Region of south China.

At the end of the nineteenth century, the Evangelical presence in Hainan remained in its infancy. Three decades had elapsed since the arrival of the enigmatic Carl Jeremiassen, and it was only 15 years since the first Presbyterian missionary reached the island. Missionary Frank Gilman reflected how the first years of mission work in Hainan were not years of ease. Without proper housing for comfortable living in a tropical climate, with no courses of study or trained teachers to assist in getting the new language, with the natives always suspicious and often unfriendly, the pioneers laid the foundations for the work.[6]

When the twentieth century commenced, the number of Chinese and tribal Christians in Hainan had reached just 57. A report in 1899 noted, "Since the establishment of the mission, 22 missionaries have been sent out, and 91 native converts added to the Church. The present missionary force is 16, and membership of the native church is 57."[7]

Although just miniscule in size, the seed of the gospel had been planted in Hainan, and like a mustard seed, it would one day grow to be a mighty tree that provided shade to multitudes of people.

A missionary selling Gospel tracts in the late nineteenth century

1900s and 1910s

A group of Hainan missionaries at Haikou, 1918

The gospel takes root

The twentieth century commenced with little progress to show for Evangelical endeavors in Hainan, with one source summarizing the progress that had been achieved in the 31 years since Carl Jeremiassen first arrived on the island:

> There were only 106 baptized Christians, no organized churches, and no ordained ministers. Why the slow growth? Perhaps the polyglot nature of the island's culture made it difficult to weld the various factions into a Christian community. Ledong was a veritable "modern day Babel," with eight different language groups within a 30-mile radius. The insular culture of the island made

it more difficult for them to relate to any outsider—foreigner or mainlander alike.[1]

For the duration of the missionary era, many recruits struggled with the linguistic complexities they faced as they tried to reach and disciple the people of Hainan. A later Presbyterian missionary, Henry Bucher, lamented,

> Since coming to Nada I have been able to do very little evangelistic work because of the "confusion of tongues." One cannot hold a boisterous crowd when speaking in a tongue they cannot understand. In Nada we are face to face with one of the most amazing dialectical jumbles in all China, if not in all the world.
>
> If this sounds like an exaggerated statement, listen to the enumeration of the different tongues common here. Every day in Nada I hear six major Chinese dialects spoken: Hakka, Lingao, Mandarin, Dan, Hainanese and Cantonese. These six major Chinese dialects, though they have some similarities, are distinctly different tongues.
>
> As if six were not enough, and to add to the confusion, we often hear the melodious monosyllables of the Li, Miao [Kim Mun] and Malaysian tongues. If this is not a "Babel" and confusion of tongues, then I do not understand the meaning of these words.[2]

While the church in other provinces of China creaked and groaned under the weight of severe persecution at the hands of the ruthless Boxer rebels in 1900, the few Christians in Hainan were largely left untouched. The small Catholic mission was targeted, however, which brought a swift call for retribution against the attackers.

Seeing how Catholic claims for compensation drove a wedge between them and the people of Hainan, Evangelical missionary Alfred Street of Haikou decided to adopt the opposite approach by refusing to be involved with any lawsuits for compensation. Street placed large placards outside his home and the chapel, declaring that Christians forgave all for the abuses of the Boxer Rebellion and would not make any claims of compensation or litigation. This stance was well received by the Hainanese, who were more receptive to the gospel from that time on.[3]

As the second decade of the new century got underway, the seed of the gospel that had been faithfully sown by the early missionaries began to take root throughout Hainan. A Presbyterian historian wrote,

> Year after year the mission schools at Ledong and Qiongzhou continued to graduate boys and girls. The Hainan Bible Institute turned out well-trained church workers. The seed sown in the preaching in the street chapels sometimes fell on fertile soil. And Dr. Henry McCandliss's 40 years' medical practice left an indelible impression.
>
> Above all, it was the personal relationships that broke down suspicion. Frank Gilman told the other missionaries that the antidote to the persistent rumors that foreigners "ate the livers and dug out people's eyes" was simply to "show yourself friendly with them and to chat about the common things of life."[4]

As a result of the persistent efforts of the missionaries, the number of Evangelical church members in Hainan grew fourfold in just eight years, increasing from just 375 in 1909 to 1,642 in 1917.[5]

One part of Hainan society that saw good progress was among the migrant laborers who traveled by ship to Southeast Asia each year for work. Many were exposed to the gospel during their time away, with one Hainan missionary noting, "Many of the Hainanese abroad have become interested in the gospel and a number who have been baptized there have come back, sought out our mission chapels, begged for teachers and evangelists to visit their homes, and have in some cases put their wives in mission schools."[6]

Boys of the Hainan Christian Middle School in 1918

The 1910s witnessed a strong surge in the number of missionary arrivals on the island. New stations were opened, and a Hakka believer named Deng Tui Vang gained the honor of being the first ordained Evangelical church leader in Hainan.

Christian work among the Hakka had commenced a generation earlier when missionaries making their way across the island came across a large settlement of Hakka people near Nada. Guo Xinxun, an elderly Chinese bookseller from Guangzhou,

> was placed among them to work for a time. He was a very zealous old man and his work resulted in securing a long list of enquirers…. In 1885, about 30 of the 60 applicants for baptism were examined and of these the rite of baptism was administered to nine and a Communion service was held—the first time the Lord's Supper was celebrated in Hainan. The sad part of it was that the zeal of the old bookseller had led him into unwise measures, and he was not only excluded from Communion but went back to Guangzhou in disgrace.[7]

Whereas the emphasis of mission work in Hainan had been on evangelism and medical missions, God's servants increasingly realized that for the gospel to transform Hainan society, Christian education needed to be one of their main priorities. Schools were opened at various places around the island, and soon hundreds of boys and girls were receiving a good Bible-based education.

Good news emerged from different areas of Hainan during the 1910s. This report told of a breakthrough in a village where strong persecution had marked the beginning of Christian work a few years earlier:

> In one village, 23 families out of 25 have become Christian. At Fong-Khom, where the first Christian, a few years ago, was persecuted and forced to pay money for exorcism, now 15 out of 30 families are Christian, and meet daily for family prayer. On Sabbaths they reach the chapel at nine in the morning and stay until four or five in the afternoon.
>
> At the village of Wakdong, a group has sprung up from a boy who came to our school and went home and taught his people. They are now preparing to build a thatched chapel. Here the Christians not only say grace before meals, but whenever they start out for work they gather for a prayer, and before starting back from their fields they have another prayer to thank God for his care. At Haobao, seven or eight families are living in shacks in the fields, because they refused to again worship the demons from whose fear they had been freed.[8]

Churches in new areas

The 1910s continued to see steady progress among Evangelical churches in Hainan, at a time when Catholic presence on the island had withered away, with just 400 Catholic believers reported in 1908.[9]

By 1915, the Presbyterians had extended their work to different parts of the province. From the start, the missionaries taught local believers to give both their time and money to God's work. This not only taught Christians the joy of being generous to others, but they also learned not to depend on foreign funding for their viability. It was hoped that this strategy would prevent the collapse of churches should the time come when missionaries were expelled from China. Missionary David Tappan reported on progress at Qionghai in eastern Hainan:

> During the past year four new chapels have been erected, three new centers opened, and the attendance at religious services has greatly increased…. We are making an every-member canvass of our Christians. We are not going to stop until we get every member to pledge a definite sum yearly or weekly.
>
> In a great many places we have more than doubled the contributions, and we have only just begun. Each Christian takes his cash and wraps it up in paper and puts his name and amount on the outside…. We expect four times as much as was given last year.[10]

The mysterious and transformative power of Jesus Christ was moving throughout Hainan, changing bad people to good, and giving a rebirth to many who were spiritually dead in their sins. Testimonies of changed lives began to emerge from villages and towns throughout the island, showing that local believers—not foreign missionaries—had become the main instruments by which people heard the message of eternal life. In 1916, this report mentioned the sacrifices of Christians in one village, providing a glimpse into the kind of persecution they were suffering for Christ:

> Two years ago in a village in Hainan there was not a Christian; now everyone in the village is a believer in Christ. They built their church with their own hands out of the material found on the mountainside. The sides of the chapel are made of bamboo poles covered with red clay. The roof is made of bamboo poles covered with fan palms. The inside walls are covered with Bible pictures and Scripture texts.

The chapel is filled every night with faithful followers of Christ. It is not an easy thing to be a worshiper of the True God in Hainan, for the Christians are scolded and reviled by their relatives and fellow villagers. Filthy abuse is heaped upon them, they are frequently robbed of their crops, and are often threatened with being driven out of the village.

In one of the schools is a Christian woman, who has been brutally treated by her husband. She has a little boy six years of age, who at Chinese New Year, when his father forced him to his knees to worship the ancestors, refused, whereupon his father struck him in the face, making it black and blue. Much prayer has been offered for the persecuted Christians, and thus far all have stood firm.[11]

Biblewomen

Many of the breakthroughs in Hainan at this time were among women, so a special emphasis was placed on discipling the island's women, almost all of whom were illiterate. Despite this challenge, the Spirit of God found many receptive hearts, and soon every mission station had sisters in Christ who were keen to share their testimony with other women. Through schools and special classes, many women were taught to read the Scriptures, and the flame of the gospel burned even brighter as a result. A 1919 report on this crucial ministry noted,

The narrow, shut-in, toil-filled lives of the women, many of whom carry heavy hearts as they go about their daily routine, respond to the message of the Savior as a plant does to the light. The training of women has been carried on ever since women missionaries came to Hainan....

In the spring of 1912, Miss Alice Skinner opened the Women's Bible School. Women who were interested in the gospel and wished to learn to read were accepted as students. Since the school was organized, 183 women have been enrolled. Many of these have learned to read, as not more than half a dozen knew a Chinese character when they entered....

Altogether, seven women have been trained as Biblewomen, six of whom are still employed, and a number more will soon be ready for work. This does not include the many others who are doing Christian work in their homes and villages.... The school has three definite aims in view—to make good earnest Christian women, to give them a good knowledge of Bible truths so that they may be able to teach others, and to train Biblewomen.[12]

The first Biblewomen at Jiangzhou (left); and Alice Skinner's Women's Bible School in 1915 (below)

Frank Gilman—the "most loved Hainan missionary"

Frank Gilman towers as one of the key lights in the history of mission work in Hainan. Born in Scottsburg, New York, in 1853, Gilman graduated from what at the time was the godly environment of Princeton University, alongside his classmate Woodrow Wilson, who went on to serve as the 28th president of the United States.

Gilman married Marion McNair in December 1885, and the couple arrived in Hainan the following year, when Frank was aged 33. He remained on the island for the next 32 years, serving his Lord and Master from 1886 to 1918. Through their holy lives and consistent Christian witness, Frank and Marion endeared themselves to many of the island's inhabitants. They were instrumental in establishing mission stations across Hainan, and Frank was described by his colleagues as "the best known and the most loved Hainan missionary."

By the early 1890s the handful of missionaries in Hainan could count just a small number of believers on the island, but in faith they looked forward to a day when the Name of Jesus Christ would be rightfully honored among all the towns and villages in Hainan. In 1890, Frank Gilman was moved to write,

> Of the 13 districts of the island, only two have had regular preaching. Of the hundreds of markets, in only two have chapels been opened. Of the thousands of villages, you can count on one hand all who have been brought under the influence of the truth. To complete the great work is the task to be performed, so that the various peoples of Hainan will be firmly united in the bonds of a living faith.... Who can tell what God will do for them, and what He will enable them to do for others?[13]

Unfortunately, Marion Gilman's life was fraught with terrible heartache and pain. She gave birth to a beloved baby daughter

Agnes who died in 1889, at just 18 months. A second daughter Flora died in Nada in 1893. The stress of these tragic experiences weighed heavily on Marion, and she was never the same again. Six years later, in 1899, Marion went to be with Christ, at the age of 44. A moving obituary provided a glimpse into the difficult struggles she had faced:

> Marion was one of the first foreign woman to meet the natives of the island, and for some time she was alone among a strange people. Only those who have passed through a similar experience can know or appreciate what a strain that was, both physically and mentally. For eight years she worked among the women of Hainan, always with enthusiasm and love, although part of the time in deep sorrow after her two oldest children were taken by the Master. Then she was in America for a furlough and returned in 1896 in seemingly good health.
>
> Early in the present year she suffered a nervous breakdown and returned with her husband and children to the United States. She so far recovered that Mr. Gilman returned to Hainan in August, expecting her to follow him next year, and now comes the news of her death.
>
> This in a few words is a bare outline of her life. But of her unselfish sweetness of character and love for the Chinese too much cannot be said.... No one has found a way to their hearts as she did. Her life was not lived out to the full, but amid sorrows and changes it was lived beautifully and well.[14]

Frank and Mary

For several years after his first wife's death, Frank Gilman threw himself into the work in Hainan. In 1903 he traveled home on furlough and married a widow, Mary, whose husband Wellington White had served as a missionary in Guangzhou for many years. After returning to Hainan, the newlyweds enjoyed over a decade of service together until Mary died at Hackensack, New Jersey, while visiting her family in September 1917.

Mary had already endured much suffering in her life. While visiting America in 1891, the wagon in which Mary, her first husband, Wellington, and their three children were riding in was struck by an express train. Wellington and their oldest daughter Lillian were instantly killed, and all the other members of the family suffered severe injuries. Mary had barely started to recover from this ordeal when her youngest child died in 1892. For several years she was unable to work as she struggled to overcome the deep physical and emotional trauma.

After Mary died in 1917, a tribute to her life said,

> Her work was characterized by conspicuous devotion, tireless activities, and an intensity of purpose that led her to put herself constantly at the disposal of the people to whom she was ministering and the missionaries with whom she was associated. She will be remembered as a faithful worker who shared with others their every burden.
>
> Not only was she faithful in her work, but her temperament was conspicuous by its buoyancy and brightness. She was especially attractive to young people. In conversation and public appeal everyone recognized the reality of her call and her devotion to the mission cause. It was not infrequent after she had finished her addresses for audiences to ask her to continue, and always at the close people would gather around her for further conversation....
>
> Her home was open to everyone—the new missionary, the tired missionary, and the missionary who needed counsel and advice.... In the latter years much of her work was done despite physical and nervous troubles to which others would have yielded; but her missionary enthusiasm was irrepressible, and one cannot help but rejoice that without a long invalidism she was called home in the midst of her work. It was as she would have wished.[15]

Having lost both his wives and living through a succession of tragedies and deaths, Frank Gilman continued to trust in the Lord Jesus and never gave up his vision to establish the kingdom of God in Hainan.

Frank Gilman in 1918, shortly before his death

Just a year following Mary's death, as rival warlords fought to gain control of Haikou in 1918, Gilman and his close coworker Henry McCandliss attempted to disarm soldiers who were hiding on the grounds of the mission hospital. In the mayhem that ensued, Gilman fell from a rock wall and sustained severe injuries, resulting in his death two weeks later. McCandliss recalled the events of his colleague's death:

> Many soldiers rushed into our compound seeking for places to hide and we disarmed them. Not knowing what to do with the arms we had taken, Mr. Gilman climbed the stone wall separating us from the British consulate to ask for instructions, but in jumping to the ground he did not alight firmly and wrenched his knee severely.
>
> After the dislocation was reduced and splintered, Mr. Gilman remained in bed for nearly three weeks. On the evening of December 3rd, we sat around his bed for an hour or more discussing the great events of the day, for the American mail had arrived, and he seemed very well in every way except for his knee. The next morning his daughter heard him call out and sent at once for me, but on my arrival he was already unconscious and died within a few minutes.
>
> In his lifetime, Frank Gilman had seen the work in Hainan grow from a hostile and contemptuous state to three well-established stations and many outstations: and from practically no adherents to many hundreds. There is something fitting that in the little foreign cemetery Mr. Jeremiassen's and Mr. Gilman's graves are side by side.[16]

Expansion

By 1917, the Hainan Mission had been spreading the gospel in Hainan for more than three decades, although Jeremiassen had arrived on the island years before the mission was formally established.

The following table shows the success of the mission from 1892 to 1917, which aligns closely to the years that Frank Gilman and his family wholeheartedly served Jesus Christ in Hainan. In many ways, Gilman towered above the mission, being involved in every branch of its activities as the work expanded to reach thousands of people.

The following statistics show a sharp increase in the number of Christian students, hospital inpatients, Christians, and adherents (those affiliated with churches who had not yet been baptized or become full church members):

Statistics for the Hainan mission[17]

Year	Christians	Adherents	Students	Inpatients
1892	78	220	74	424
1900	106	265	86	391
1909	375	1,187	281	673
1917	1,642	3,535	1,500	2,972

1920s

A mission hub for Hainan

The town of Jiangzhou, just a few miles from the provincial capital Haikou, was chosen as the headquarters for much of the mission work in Hainan. It grew over time, becoming the base for a hospital, Bible school, churches, and Christian schools. From

Haikou Church in the 1920s

65

Jiangzhou, the gospel radiated out to cover the whole island. A 1919 mission book, written by Frank Gilman, detailed some of the successes and challenges faced by the workers at Jiangzhou:

> The missionaries lived outside the city wall in Jiangzhou, suffering from heat and malarial fevers, crowded and dirty streets, and the multitudinous odors of a Chinese city. Gradually, however, the station settled in three compounds.... The early days of hospital work, when the doctor scarcely dared to perform an amputation for fear of the mob that might arise, and the present time...are vastly different.[1]

The 1920s saw tumultuous times for Christians in Hainan, with competing warlords and mobs of bloodthirsty bandits wreaking havoc on the population as they raped, burned, and murdered their way across the island. Among the chaos, however, the kingdom of God continued to shine, with stories emerging of how people were responding to and being transformed by the gospel. As an example, missionary John Steiner shared this testimony in 1925:

> A certain man had never heard a sermon or attended a religious service. Through our evangelist, a copy of the Bible fell into his hands. This was read over and over, and he became convinced of its truth. Today he is saturated with its teachings. He quotes text after text, is familiar with both the Old and the New Testament and finds chapter and verse without the use of a concordance. Best of all, he has been instrumental in leading 18 of his villagers to become Christians, and they have built their own chapel. His house is at the roadside, and he always has some interesting direct gospel message posted up for the benefit of those passing by.[2]

Medical work continued to be the main way people were exposed to the teachings of Christ, with the Presbyterians continuing to run the only hospital on the island. The missionaries were under great strain for much of the time, as they strove to treat thousands of people with various ailments, while they constantly struggled to obtain adequate supplies. In a summary of a typical year, the Presbyterian hospital treated 2,859 in-patients, "of which 739 were maternity cases and 580 were surgical operations. The patients came chiefly from northeast Hainan."[3]

Crossroads for medical missions

The hospital earned such a good reputation that patients from mainland China regularly crossed the strait to receive treatment in Jiangzhou.

By the late 1920s, however, the missionaries were faced with a difficult decision. The Chinese government expressed their desire to build and operate their own hospital in Hainan, to cater to the island's burgeoning population. Almost all the medical workers on the island had been trained by the Presbyterians, and they could not pay the doctors and nurses anywhere near the level being offered by the government.

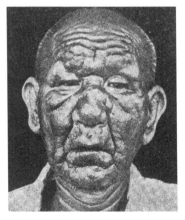 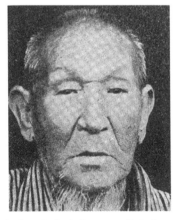

Medical work continued to be the main thrust of missionary activity in Hainan. This man suffering from nodular leprosy was treated, with remarkable results as the before-and-after photos show

The dilemma for the missionaries lay in the fact that from the very beginning of Evangelical work in Hainan, their medical work had been accompanied by the preaching of the gospel, and the government now wanted to take over the medical part of the work while rejecting the spiritual aspect. It caused one American missionary-doctor, Nathaniel Bercovitz, to seek God for direction. He wrote,

> How far should this hospital undertake public health work? The problems are extremely practical.... The ultimate purpose of medical missionary work is active extension of Christianity through medical work. This includes the pioneer type of work, as well as every other type of medical work. Without this purpose, the field might as well be left to other medical agencies serving only humanitarian and scientific purposes. But the time should never come when a mission hospital can cease to be an active evangelizing agency, as well as a medical center....
>
> Christian missions mean the proclamation of the direct gospel message; but the work includes living the Christian life in every phase and relationship, and in good deeds which are the fruit of the Spirit....
>
> In all the rooms of the Haikou Hospital are placed Bibles, and Bible texts are printed on the walls. It is not unusual for an educated patient to read through the Bible while in the hospital and many ask for copies on leaving. One man, whose wife had a very serious surgical operation, said that one night when her condition was the lowest, he never took his eyes off the text on the wall: "God is our refuge and strength, a very present help in time of trouble."[4]

In the end, the missionaries decided they must continue to honor Christ by keeping the proclamation of the gospel at the forefront of everything they did. They continued to run their mission hospital and medical clinics, while the government opened theirs.

Several years later, Bercovitz shared this testimony to show the effectiveness of their approach:

> A man came to the hospital with a surgical condition and was cured. The evangelist sat with him, and when the patient left, he was given some tracts and a Bible.
>
> Months later the pastor of the Haikou church visited the region where this patient lived and was invited to visit his village. The pastor was amazed to find a group of 94 people asking for baptism in a village where no evangelist had ever gone, and where the only work had been done through this one patient in the hospital. The pastor felt that 61 of these candidates were ready to be baptized. Since that time many have had to endure persecution, but a recent visit brought word that the group was standing firm, forming a strong Christian nucleus in their village.[5]

George and Clara Byers

After George Byers and his family arrived in Hainan in 1906, they gained widespread respect as quiet, godly believers who desired that all people should walk in the light and truth of Jesus Christ.

Every Christmas, Byers—a native of Nova Scotia but a naturalized citizen of the United States—liked to write an account of all the things God had led him to do in the past year. In 1924 he wrote, "We do not know how long we may live or what we shall meet with in life…. My chief desire is to always do those things that please Him."[6]

As the social situation deteriorated in Hainan, Byers detailed the worsening conditions in a letter to his home church, in what turned out to be one of his final communications:

> Many of our members have suffered…. Some have lost their lives and others have been captured and held for ransom. About two months ago the home of one of our well-to-do members was

broken into and the head of the family carried off. He has just obtained his release by paying $800.[7]

On June 24, 1924, George Byers was walking home from a prayer meeting at the Qionghai Hospital when four armed men, seeking ransom money, seized the missionary and dragged him down the road with a rope fastened around his neck.

When Byers' 10-year-old son Robert heard the barking of the family dog he went outside to investigate. Fearing the commotion would soon attract more unwanted attention, the bandits opened fire and George Byers was shot several times. A bullet grazed Robert's leg but he managed to raise the alarm, but by the time help arrived, his 50-year-old father lay dead.

George Byers early in his missionary career

A detailed account of the botched kidnapping said,

It should have been easy: there were three of them and only one missionary. The kidnappers lay in wait. Byers came. The kidnappers sprang into action, slipped a noose around their victim's neck, and then disaster—Byers struggled violently to get free, and shouted for his wife to help him. No one dreamed he would try to fight three men. But fight he did, and in the melee, the gun, pressed tight against the missionary's abdomen, went off.

In an instant, the planned kidnapping became murder. Then Mrs. Byers and Robert appeared, something else the kidnappers had not planned on. The culprits fled into the darkness of the Chinese countryside, never stopping to retrieve the ransom note. They had not expected this—a dead foreigner and no ransom.[8]

Clara Byers, a pregnant mother of four and in a state of shock, had no option but to notify the mission community in Haikou and the authorities about the murder of her husband. Her simple letter, written with a shaking hand, read, "Four ruffians entered the compound to bind and carry off Mr. Byers. He refused to go so was shot in the abdomen and killed. Tell the others. Please come at once to Qionghai to make arrangements for burial."[9]

The Hainan mission community had suffered a heavy loss, with one publication describing Byers as quiet, conscientious, standing with unwavering fidelity for what is right,

and devoted to the task of bringing the Good News of the kingdom to the people of Hainan. A man of prayer and of deep spiritual discernment, the Mission, the Church, and the Chinese among whom he worked have sustained almost an irreparable loss in his death. The Li and Kim Mun work in the Qionghai field was very dear to him, and he often exhausted his physical strength in the itinerating trips he made. Our deepest sympathy goes out to the stricken family, who has lost a devoted husband and father.[10]

Before arriving in Hainan in 1906, George Byers' diary had recorded his dissatisfaction at the small number of people he had been able to lead to Christ in the United States. During the following years, however, "[h]e had his prayer answered in the hundreds whom he was permitted to baptize in Qionghai. The love of the people for their pastor was shown…as believers inquire if it could be true that their pastor had been killed. Tears filled their eyes as they told of his kind deeds."[11]

It is fitting that the last words on George Byers were written by the missionary himself. In a report that had yet to be published before his death, he told of the stunning progress of work in Qionghai, which had grown to become the largest and most influential church in Hainan. The martyr wrote,

> The gospel is spreading from the Kim Mun people to the Li people near the Five Finger Mountains [Wuzhishan]. A young man was married there whose grandfather, after four years of blindness, had his sight restored by the removal of cataracts from his eyes at the Qionghai Hospital. This old gentleman so rejoiced to have his sight that he immediately acknowledged Jesus as his Savior….
>
> Christianity is slowly winning its way into this home. There have been ten Communion services in Qionghai since the last mission meeting. At these services, 408 applicants for baptism were examined by the session, and 236 were taken into the Church.[12]

George Byers was buried in the foreign cemetery, a short distance from the grave of the first Evangelical on the island, Carl Jeremiassen. Byers' death was a particular blow to the fledgling Kim Mun tribal Christians, many of whom considered him their "spiritual father."

Clara's pain of suddenly becoming a widow with five fatherless children to take care of was exacerbated when the American Presbyterian Mission did little to help or encourage her.

Clara Byers, who was abandoned in the time of her greatest need

With only her missionary friend Mabel Roys offering any real assistance, Clara found her cries for help and justice were blocked by her own mission board, which seemed more concerned about saving money than supporting Clara and her grieving children in a remote mission station. Scholar Kathleen Lodwick explained the outrageous and cowardly stance adopted by the Presbyterian leaders in New York:

> Its members felt it had no responsibility to support Mrs. Byers and her family, once they were no longer on the mission field. The members took their position because their contributors gave money for the support of foreign missions, not for the maintenance of those widowed and orphaned on the field. Yet they also insisted Mrs. Byers could not claim the indemnity from the

American government as a missionary, since that action could jeopardize future mission work in China....

With five children, the oldest only 11, Mrs. Byers had few options. Her own parents were dead as were her husband's. Her only siblings were two half-brothers, both married, and neither likely to want to have six more people to support.[13]

Even though the identities of the murderers were known, no arrests were ever made in the death of George Byers.

In the end, Clara did receive a modest sum to help her family adjust to life in America. It did not come from the Presbyterian Mission, however, but was procured after US senators and congressmen got involved in a bid to provide a measure of justice to the grieving family. The board of the Presbyterian Mission, shaken by the chorus of criticism that engulfed them, belatedly offered Clara a modest pension.

The missionary endeavor in Hainan suffered another harsh blow five months after the death of George Byers, when William Stinson died in a sawmill accident as he was overseeing the construction of new mission buildings.

These setbacks shocked the mission community, but a relative calm prevailed for the next two years until anti-Christian sentiment exploded at Qionghai in 1926, as part of wider anti-Christian demonstrations throughout China that year. A mission magazine reported,

In Hainan, at a place where Mr. Byers of the American Presbyterian Mission was murdered about two years ago, a mob of about 1,000 attacked the hospital and beat up the native workers and drove them away. Some damage was done and the gate was broken down and [there were] other minor damages.... The colleges, primary schools, the missionaries' homes etc., have been seized by the military and it is reported the missionaries have been driven out.[14]

Attendees at the 1923 Hainan Mission conference

By the late 1920s the missionary community in Hainan had grown to become a small yet effective presence, providing spiritual salt and light to people throughout the island.

In 1922 a groundbreaking book, *The Christian Occupation of China* was published. It detailed the most comprehensive research available on the state of the church in China at the time. The book included the first detailed snapshot of Evangelical Christianity in Hainan, with a summary presented in the table below:[15]

Evangelicals in Hainan, 1922

Location	Population	Work Started	Churches	Preaching Centers	Total Christians
Qiongshan	440,000	1881	0	10	266
Chengmai	42,480	1910	0	2	193
Ding'an	49,560	1899	0	4	183
Wenchang	360,000	1910	0	5	210

Location	Popula-tion	Work Started	Church-es	Preach-ing Centers	Total Chris-tians
Qiongzhong	85,000	1900	1	3	311
Qionghai	80,000	1916	0	1	2
Lingao	48,680	–	0	4	80
Danzhou	160,000	1888	3	3	355
Sanya	80,000	1890	–	–	–
Wanning	310,746	1906	0	5	105
Lingshui	95,000	1917	0	1	0
Changjiang	35,362	–	–	–	–
Gancheng	32,680	–	–	–	–
TOTALS	1,819,508		4	38	1,705

By the close of the 1920s the work in Hainan had further matured and expanded. In 1927, the statistics for the Presbyterian Mission on the island were as follows: "Three ordained ministers, eight organized churches, 4,075 communicant members, 24 primary schools, two high schools, three hospitals (240 beds), 1,707 in-patients, and 22,127 out-patients."[16]

Despite the encouraging progress, the body of Christ was being stretched in new directions. Society in Hainan and across China had been in turmoil for decades, and debates were being held about what form of government, society, and church the Chinese people needed going forward.

In a 1926 survey, 170 Chinese Christians were asked how the church in China could be improved. In their shocking responses are seen the seeds for the registered church structure that was later introduced by the Communist Party to control Christianity in China. Responses to the survey included these suggestions: "Shatter denominationalism; Hand church authority to the

Chinese; Let the church promote industry and savings institutions; Get rid of capitalism and class distinctions; Use scientific methods in preaching; Co-operate with other agencies in social work; Respect foreign missionaries who come to serve, but send the arrogant ones home."[17]

Interestingly, although more than a quarter century was to pass until the official founding of the Three-Self Patriotic Movement in 1954, the character of the movement included all the features voiced by the 170 responders in 1926.

1930s

A group of missionaries at Qionghai in 1934

A turbulent decade

Banditry and lawlessness continued to plague the people of Hainan throughout the 1930s, with many Christians suffering at the hands of violent men. Despite the great difficulties, missionary work continued, with many emissaries of Christ displaying tremendous courage as they faithfully served people on the island.

Margaret Melrose, a veteran missionary whose long career was winding down, served in Hainan for 43 years from 1890 to 1933. A native of Iowa, the furthest she had ever traveled from home was to attend the state fair in Des Moines before she volunteered to be a missionary to unreached people on the other side of the world.

Margaret and her husband, John Melrose, commenced work at Nada in 1890. Seven years later their precious infant daughter Esther died of fever, bringing great distress and sorrow to John and Margaret. The agony weighed so heavily on John that he suffered a gastric hemorrhage and died just 13 days later, aged 38.

Reeling from such a crippling double blow, everyone assumed Margaret would return to America and lead a quiet life. Margaret confounded them, however, by leaving her two sons in the care of her sister and returned to Hainan to continue the work alone. For years she taught literacy classes and often traveled on difficult month-long journeys by horseback into the wild interior mountains, where few Chinese dared to venture.

For many years Margaret bravely continued to share God's love with the Li and Kim Mun tribes, using local interpreters to communicate with them. She conducted regular medical clinics for the impoverished people, many of whom were dying before the age of 40 because of disease and lack of hygiene. Her tireless dedication and selfless service won the admiration of all who knew her.

After nearly half a century in Hainan, Melrose retired to America in 1933 and went to be with the Lord in 1951, aged 83. When she retired, the Presbyterian Mission wrote this stirring tribute to her:

> With an iron physique and will to match, she has moved mountains, crossed oceans, suffered the deepest sorrows and loneliness, counted discomforts as nothing—all to make known the kingdom of God in Hainan. No one can estimate the villages that are changed or the lives she has touched because she left all and followed Him to the uttermost parts.[1]

Margaret Melrose's influence among the people of Hainan lived on when her son Paul and his wife, Esther, returned to the land of his birth in 1916. They served on the island until it was overrun by the Communists in 1951. Their daughter, Marie Melrose, carried on the great spiritual heritage by serving as a missionary to South Korea and later China.

Marie Melrose (second from right) with Christian friends
during a visit to Hainan in the 1980s
Bridge

Communism vs Christianity

As the 1930s progressed, Mao Zedong led the Communists
to many victories during the Chinese civil war, and it became
increasingly apparent that they would gain control of all of China
unless they suffered unexpected setbacks. In 1926, Marxist agitators from the Soviet Union dubbed Hainan, "A Laboratory of
Communism," because of its isolation. They wanted to use the
island as a testing ground for the implementation of their atheistic ideologies but were incensed by the presence of growing
Christian communities throughout the island. A 1931 article
spoke about the spiritual and ideological clash that was underway
between Communism and Christianity in Hainan at the time:

> Communists, both Russian and Chinese, have sought by indoctri-
> nation, intimidation, misrepresentation, and worse, to make the

island Communist. A campaign of terrorism forced the evacuation of many members of the mission for one or two years. Finally, the government expelled the worst agitators, but only temporarily as they are again active. Few roads are safe for travel; block houses line the hilltops along the highways; and towns and villages are under constant guard.

Here is an excellent opportunity to make the island a "Laboratory of Christianity." The Presbyterians are the only mission at work there. The president of the Chamber of Commerce recently said, "Hainan is deeply grateful for the effective and sacrificial service of the American missionaries, and we want them to stay forever."[2]

The Lingao people

The Lingao (formerly spelled "Limko") people are the second largest Chinese group in Hainan, after the Hainanese-speaking Chinese. Numbering around 700,000 people, they primarily inhabit counties in the north of the island in and around the city

Lingao fishermen heading out on the beautiful waters of the Longbo Bay
Zuma Press

of Lingao. Although the Chinese government was quick to place the Lingao ethnic group under the Han nationality, historical records considered them Li people. While many Lingao today are bilingual in other Chinese vernaculars, their heart language is, like Li, part of the Tai family.

The first Lingao Christians date back to the earliest years of nineteenth-century mission work on the island, but a wonderful breakthrough occurred in the 1930s, resulting in hundreds of people surrendering their lives to Jesus Christ despite the grim conditions in society caused by famine, lawlessness, and war.

In 1936, American missionary Paul Melrose summarized the progress and trials of the Lingao church to that point in time, under the leadership of Pastor Fu Vun Khai:

> The Lingao are found in a district 50 miles (81 km) and more west of Hainan's one treaty-port, Haikou. In ancient times this tribe probably drifted over from mainland Asia, since their language has much in common with that of the Laos of Siam [now Thailand]. Less than a generation ago the Lingao first heard the gospel, and since then they have come into the Christian Church in increasing numbers....
>
> During the dark days of 1926–27 the Lingao Christians were subjected to bitter persecution. Anti-Christian papers were pasted on the chapel walls; efforts were made to prevent worship meetings; the townspeople said it was time to "take back" church property; and the Communists openly used the chapel for a primary school.
>
> Finally, the Reds seized the town of Lingao and made it a Communistic center. A few days later the tide turned, however. Loyalists drove out the Reds and the church was again occupied by the Christians. The next year they bought a new piece of land and, after self-sacrificing effort, built a fine new chapel....
>
> For three years the rains failed, and the rice rose in price until the poor Lingaos could not afford to buy. They made sweet potatoes (known in Hainan as the "bread of poverty") the staple

of their diet. Then war came and brought ruin in its train. The Communists fortified a nearby village and made that their headquarters until government troops dislodged them. After the battle, the village of 1,000 homes was obliterated and the inhabitants were either killed, captured, or scattered. Nearly 100 destitute Christians found refuge in the chapel....

During all this period the Lingaos never lost sight of their goal, and in October 1931, a new house of worship was dedicated.... This new group of about 200 members is an offshoot of Pastor Fu's congregation. The Lingao of Hainan are coming into the kingdom of God.[3]

In 2019, the Lingao New Testament was finally completed, allowing the people of this precious group to have the Word of God in their heart language for the first time in history. Today there are an estimated 28,000 Lingao Christians, or approximately four percent of their population.[4]

Henry and Louise Bucher

Throughout the 1930s, new Presbyterian missionaries continued to trickle into Hainan. Among them were Henry and Louise Bucher, who arrived in Nada in 1934.

Henry, a graduate from Princeton Seminary, was from New Jersey, and Louise hailed from Virginia. Just months after their arrival, Louise gave birth to their first child, Anna, at Haikou. In March 1936 they had a son, Henry Jr., and in June the following year twin daughters, Priscilla (known as Pril) and Dorothy were born as Japanese bombs fell all around them. With stress and chaos engulfing the island, Dorothy was stillborn. Pril's delivery was complicated and she was born with cerebral palsy, but went on to live 77 years and brought joy to many people.

In 1939, Henry found himself running the Presbyterian mission when the full Japanese invasion occurred. He wrote

Henry and Louise Bucher

this report, which offered a glimpse into the body of Christ in Hainan at the time:

> Altogether this unspeakable war has made inroads upon our strength and energy—and nerves. In all my life I have never experienced so sustained a drain upon my energies, both mental and physical, as during this past year....
>
> I am the only male missionary in this part of Hainan, and have charge of the employees and of all property and repairs of the large compound.... My major missionary role is superintendent of all the evangelistic work in Nada, with a dozen churches and a congregation of several thousand. I am the treasurer for all the

evangelists in this area, and pastor of six of the country churches which have a combined congregation of 2,000.

I am also responsible for the Lodi field in the mountainous interior where there are 2,500 professed believers awaiting instruction.[5]

The Buchers served the people of Hainan with all their energy and gifts, but the Japanese occupation intensified, and Henry, Louise, and their children were arrested and interned at a Japanese prisoner of war camp.

While Louise and the children were treated respectfully, Henry underwent frequent interrogations designed to break his mind and spirit. Years later, as they awaited repatriation home to the United States in 1945, Louise wrote a letter to Henry's parents, in which she tried to share the seriousness of her husband's condition without causing distress to Henry's parents. Louise wrote,

Can you imagine what home mail means to us after being cut off for so long? We have so enjoyed hearing from you and many others....

We are all improving on this good nourishing food except Henry.... He is terribly nervous, so thin and pale. I can't help but be anxious about him. He can't seem to relax. The internment experience was harder for him than any of us. I do hope and pray he will calm down and take it easy. I think when we get started home maybe he will be better....

Most of our things are lost. All our precious mementos are happy memories. But we are thankful to be alive. We can start all over again just as we did when we were first married. It will be fun. This time we want fewer but better things in clothes and equipment. Henry got here with one pair of trousers, no pajamas and a couple of shirts. The children have gone barefooted so long they don't mind but we hope to get shoes before we start for home. This is particularly important for Pril....

> There are thousands of things we want to tell you. It is better not to write them. We know the prayers of our friends and loved ones saved us. It is truly miraculous.[6]

The Buchers finally reached the United States in May 1945, a few months before the war ended when the US dropped atomic bombs on Hiroshima and Nagasaki. Henry and Louise enrolled to study at Hartford Seminary.

Friends and family of the Buchers were glad they were finally "safe" at home, but the pioneer spirit was planted deep within Henry and Louise. After the Japanese were repelled, the Nationalist government did a survey of Hainan and when they asked the people what they needed to rebuild, they responded, "We need the Christian missionaries to come back." General Chiang Kai-shek issued an order, asking for those missionaries who had been expelled by the Japanese to return to the island.

The Buchers often wondered how their Christian friends in Hainan were doing, and when they heard General Chiang's request, they realized they would only experience God's full peace and blessing if they obeyed His call on their lives. At the end of 1946, Henry and Louise returned to Hainan for another term of service.

Henry continued to struggle with his health, and after a bout of amoebic dysentery hospitalized him in 1949, doctors advised the Buchers to return to the United States permanently. They settled in New Jersey and worked with the Presbyterian Board of Christian Education for the next seven years, but once again the call to the Far East caused them to accept a position in Thailand, where they served from 1956 to 1972.

Their years in Thailand were not without intense trials. In 1964, their daughter Pril, who was 27 at the time, suffered severe burns when her clothes caught fire. After carrying the heavy burden of caring for their beloved daughter as she lived with cerebral palsy, this incident almost broke the Buchers, but they surrendered their lives afresh to God and moved forward in daily faith.

After full lives marked by their dedicated service to God and excruciating trials, Louise finally went to her eternal reward in 1996, aged 88, with Henry following two years later, at the age of 91.

Although few people ever heard of the Bucher family and their sacrificial service on Hainan Island, many Chinese, Li, and Kim Mun believers will rise up on judgment day and call them blessed.

Startling growth

The extensive 1922 survey of Evangelical Christians in China had reported 1,705 believers in Hainan, but the church was energized by the Holy Spirit, and the following decade witnessed a rapid increase in the number of Christians.

By 1927, just five years after that landmark survey, the number of Evangelical believers in Hainan had more than doubled to 4,078,[7] and by the early 1930s that number had edged up to 5,000.[8]

Decades later, a trustworthy Chinese Christian publication, based on interviews with key Hainan church leaders, estimated there had been 10,000 Evangelical Christians in Hainan in 1930.[9]

Whatever the true figure, Christianity in Hainan had clearly shaken off its marginalized stigma and had begun to enter the mainstream of society, with peasants and university students alike deeply contemplating the teachings of Jesus Christ. The future looked bright for the gospel in China's southernmost province.

The Kim Mun

A misidentified tribe

Approximately 80,000 people in Hainan officially belong to China's Miao nationality. The ancestors of this group migrated from mainland China to Hainan at least 400 years ago. The Chinese living on the island at the time immediately labeled them "Miao," as at that time almost all tribal people in south China were either described as "Miao" or "Lolo," and each group's distinctiveness was considered irrelevant.

A Kim Mun woman in central Hainan
Thomas Boehm

When missionaries in the early twentieth century encountered these "Miao," they were baffled as to why their language and customs appeared to be totally different from Miao people on the mainland. It was because they were not Miao at all, though the Chinese government continues to classify them as Miao to the present day.

In reality, the "Miao" people of Hainan are part of a tribe called the Kim Mun. More than 200,000 Kim Mun live in south China's Guangxi and Yunnan provinces, where, oddly, the government has classified them as a subgroup of the Yao nationality. A smaller number of Kim Mun are also found outside China in north Vietnam and Laos.

The Kim Mun language is not part of the Miao family, nor are their customs and history related to the Miao. Ironically, when communicating with outsiders, it seems that over the course of many generations the Kim Mun in Hainan have come to adopt the name the Chinese have long called them, so that many of the people themselves appear to have grudgingly accepted the label of being Miao, having grown tired of trying to insist on their own identity.

It is important for Christians to classify this precious group accurately, for several reasons. If a Miao evangelist comes from mainland China, they would quickly discover the Kim Mun speak a completely different language from their own, and would face almost as many cross-cultural and linguistic barriers to the gospel as any other race attempting to reach them.

Furthermore, Christian resources created to reach these people in Hainan need to be specific to the Kim Mun people. They need to hear the gospel of Jesus Christ in their heart language, and efforts to reach them using Chinese, or a Miao language, will not penetrate deeply into the hearts and minds of the people. Christian Scripture that has already been translated into several Miao languages and used elsewhere in China is completely useless in the hands of a Kim Mun person. For these reasons, this precious people group have been referred to by their correct name, Kim Mun, in this book.

From the time they arrived in Hainan, the Kim Mun found themselves living in many of the same areas as the Li, who are recognized as the original inhabitants of the island. For generations the Li bullied the shy Kim Mun, oppressing them and frequently reverting to violence, including headhunting when disputes between the two tribes escalated.

Missionaries initially contacted the Kim Mun in the 1880s, although it seems they were never specifically targeted with the gospel due to language difficulties. As a result, the Kim Mun received no more than a fleeting witness. Missionary reports offered only occasional passing references to the Kim Mun. For example, in 1917 the Presbyterian missionary Margaret Moninger wrote,

> A tribe of Li has come out and have taken a Kim Mun man and bound him and carried him off because as they say, there has been a sickness in the Li villages, and the Kim Mun have built their chapel in a place that disturbs the grave of a Li ancestor.[1]

In 1938 when explorer Leonard Clark crossed Hainan, he was shocked to come across a Kim Mun village in the geographical center of the island. Clark wrote in *National Geographic*,

> I stumbled across a "Lost Valley," surrounded by tall pines rooted in red dirt. The inhabitants were not Lis! I soon learned that they were Miao [Kim Mun] who had migrated here from South China probably hundreds of years before.
>
> Finding the valley unoccupied, they had made a treaty with the surrounding Li, built a village from the giant bamboo in the valley, and, like the true pioneers that they were, begun work on paddy terraces on nearby slopes. Now they lived here happily and in peace....

These were the first people we had encountered who could read; for hundreds of years, from father to son, the language of China had been taught! They still wore queues [long braided hair] and were amazed to learn that China was no longer ruled by the Manchus.[2]

A hunting accident brings a blessing

One day in the autumn of 1914, a bear mauled a Kim Mun peasant named Chen Riguang while he was out hunting. Chen's head, arm and right eye were badly torn by the beast, but he somehow managed to make his way to the Gospel Hospital in Jiaji. He recovered after staying there for six weeks.

As Chen's wounds gradually healed, Chinese evangelists Wu Yixin and Feng Huanxin visited him and lovingly shared the gospel. Chen was touched by their genuine concern and welcomed the Savior into his heart. He was given a Bible and other Christian books.

When Chen returned to his home village of Xincun, his family and friends were amazed to see the change that had taken place in his life. After hearing what had happened, the villagers traveled to the Gospel Hospital to experience the loving kindness of the Christians for themselves.

By the end of 1915, more than 300 families in 17 Kim Mun villages in the Nanmao district had turned to Christ. The number of Christians grew rapidly, and Chinese Bible teachers were sent to help disciple the new believers.

A chief's dream

A different account of how the Kim Mun came to faith in Jesus was told by Presbyterian missionaries. According to them, in 1916 a Kim Mun chief, Zit-kwang, had a terrible dream where he saw his house in the blackest darkness, before it was illuminated by a great light. The dream terrified the chief, for the Kim Mun believed that

> when bad people die they go to a terrible place, their perception of hell—a thick, dark forest with no villages or clearings. They believe that good people will go to one of several levels of heaven, depending on how much care their eldest son gave the spirit of his dead parent.[3]

The chief's dream was so powerful that he immediately visited the Jiaji Mission station, where he begged the missionaries to help his people come out of darkness and into the light. The missionaries visited the chief's village and brought back this astonishing report:

Some of the first Kim Mun Christian women in the 1920s
Katherine Schaeffer

After our first visit to this village, his people built a thatched chapel and our Chinese evangelist soon reported throngs of people, from many miles around, coming every Sunday to learn of the Christian God. Some days nearly 1,000 Kim Mun would meet, and it was very hard to hold an orderly meeting with people so new and strange.

When they had learned a few lessons in the worship of the true God they returned home, and village after village built a chapel of their own, assembling every morning and evening to sing hymns, read the New Testament, and pray. I asked one village chief how many families in his village worshipped God. "All of them," he replied. "When we built the chapel two families refused to join with us and so they moved to another village."[4]

Kim Mun believers begged missionary Margaret Moninger to open schools in their area so they could learn to read and write. She wrote in 1917, "We feel we are having wonderful opportunities for the spread of the gospel here, with the Li first and now the Kim Mun literally begging for the message."[5]

The Kim Mun and other Christians in the mountains of Hainan developed a unique custom where they organized what they dubbed "Big Sundays." Twice a year all the Christians in an area gathered for several days of festivities, where they would be instructed in the Word of God and enjoy fellowship. In a book edited by Moninger, she described a typical Big Sunday gathering:

It is indeed an inspiration to see the Christians come in—men, women, and children—some by boat and some by road, some having walked 25 or 30 miles. Services are held in the chapel morning and evening, special classes for women are carried on, and the members of the session are kept busy examining candidates. In fact, all of us are kept busy finding places for the crowds to sleep, hearing of the sorrows and joys of our flock, giving a word of warning here or of encouragement there....

The climax, to us all, is the baptism of the new members of the Church of Christ, and then the Communion together."[6]

Kim Mun Christian girls reading the Bible at Nanmao in 1988
Bridge

A poem for the Kim Mun

Missionary-doctor J. Franklin Kelly served among the Kim Mun, treating their bodies as well as their spiritual needs. In 1915 he penned a poem in their honor, which he entitled "The Miao Men of China,"[7] in which he detailed the events that led to thousands of Kim Mun people becoming Christians. Kelly wrote,

The Miao Men of China

We have met the Miao men,
Simple children of the forest,
From the mountains of the mainland,
Who are strangers in our island,

They have journeyed up the rivers,
Climbed up high into the mountains,
Finding homes within the jungle—
There they burn down woods and thickets,

The Kim Mun

Making ashes for their gardens,
Growing corn, hill-rice, and tubers....

We would tell of their brave chieftain,
Of the lettered brave's adventures....
Then he came to mission doctor—
Got his face patched, heard the Gospel.
He it was who had the vision
Of a white light in his dwelling,

Then, with spirit deeply troubled,
Came again unto the white men
For more light and we all told him
Light in this dark world is Jesus,
Savior of all tribes and nations.

Then returned he to his tribesmen—
Zit-kwang, the patch-face chieftain—
Sent out letters to his people,
Summoned them from all the mountains,
Gathered them from all the forests.

Lo they came by scores and fifties,
Sixties and the hundreds. Thousands
Now are listening to the good news;
All are having dreams and visions,
Dancings, shakings and upheavals,
Fiercest strugglings with their demons.

Then they gave up homes and treasures,
Came out fully in the open
Light of day with swift fulfilment
Of the vision of the prophets;

Now they've built a new pavilion
Where they gather to their worship,
To their reading of the Gospel,
To their prayers and singing hymns.

Chen Riguang's slide into error

By the start of the 1920s, Christianity among the Kim Mun appeared to have divided into two groups: the Presbyterians and a second group led by Chen Riguang, the man who first believed in Christ after being mauled by a bear. According to some sources, Chen was voted the Christian leader of the Kim Mun. In the summer of 1920, at his direction, a large building was erected in Xincun to serve as the main church center for the whole district.

Although Chen was zealous for the faith, his understanding of biblical Christianity proved superficial, and a wiser choice of leader may have prevented the terrible error that many Kim Mun Christians soon embraced. Chen's slide into error appears to have accelerated after he met a Daoist priest, who convinced him that the Christian God was the same as Pan Wang, the mythical deity the Kim Mun consider the progenitor and hero of their race.

The normally placid Margaret Moninger, who loved the Kim Mun and desired to see them glorify Christ, wrote this blunt evaluation of Chen Riguang:

> I verily believe that he is a consummate rascal. He certainly was the instrument used of the Lord to open the work here, but he apparently did his share with the desire to get glory for himself. Now that the people are learning the truth and not following his false ways, he is trying in every way to work against the church by all sorts of tricks and yet to Mr. Byers or any of the rest of us he talks like a saint…. But he is gradually losing influence in every village except his own.[8]

After Chen declared that the Second Coming of Christ was imminent, many Christians sold their cattle and stopped working in the fields as they waited for the event to occur. When it didn't eventuate, many Kim Mun families faced starvation and became disillusioned with Christianity. Unfortunately, Chen then went from bad to worse. He reportedly

> appointed 12 elders in 12 churches. They wore long robes and stood at his side during services. He himself sat on a raised seat in the center and called himself the "King of Peace." Believers were required to kneel down and worship him on the 1st and 15th days of every lunar month.... Consequently, nearly half of his followers left the church. But, at the same time, many newcomers arrived to replace them.[9]

In the end, a measure of peace came to the sincere followers of Christ when Chen moved out of the district. He constructed a temple on Diaoluo Mountain, the highest peak in the Wuzhi Range, where he "appointed a Counselor and five Prime Ministers to govern the area."[10]

Chinese church leaders heard about these dire events and tried to counter Chen's influence by starting a free Christian school at Yangzhu village. Some Kim Mun people, however, felt they had been burned by "Christianity" and were unwilling to embrace it as they once had.

From "human soup" to followers of Jesus

Despite the setbacks, God continued to bless His remnant among the Kim Mun. In 1927, Hugh Bousman of the Presbyterian Mission in Qionghai shared some interesting experiences he had with Kim Mun people. One man told him,

> "Once, robbers attacked our village. We killed one of them. According to our custom we took some of his bones and made soup and each of us ate a little of it." This man is the headman of a little Kim Mun village of 10 or 15 families.
>
> Many of these people are now Christians. On a recent trip to visit them, we sat on the side of a high mountain. Before us, in the little pocket-like valley on the mountainside were the

mud-daubed and leaf-thatched houses of the villagers. Beside us was the village chapel we had come to visit. These Kim Mun Christians…come morning and evening to have prayers and to sing before they go to their work or to bed.[11]

Another decade passed until 1937, when American missionary David Tappan told of a Kim Mun Communion service he attended high in the remote mountains of central Hainan: "Nearly 100 mountain folks caught a glimpse of their Lord that day, and somehow I feel that He was as much at home at that makeshift table than at any Communion service in America with their perfect appointments."[12]

In 1943, the Nationalist army was told that the Kim Mun living around the Wuzhi Mountains had collaborated with the Japanese army (when in fact they had been forced at gunpoint to carry provisions for them). An order was issued to exterminate all Kim Mun in the area, and approximately 2,000 people living in more than 30 villages in Nanmao, Luping, and Jialue were slaughtered. This represented 40 percent of the total Kim Mun population in Hainan at the time. Many of the dead were those who had earlier joined the church.

Although Chen Riguang and his son were among those killed, their heresies continued to exert a poisonous influence among the Kim Mun for decades. The temple he built on Diaoluo Mountain is still recognized as a sacred place by most Kim Mun people today.

Today's Kim Mun Christians

With such an unstable spiritual foundation due to the influence of Chen Riguang and other church leaders, it is unsurprising that when Communist persecution arrived in the 1960s and 1970s the Kim Mun churches were decimated, and many believers quickly fell away. One source noted, "In the 1930s the Kim Mun

A Kim Mun choir worshipping in a Three-Self church in 1992
Bridge

tribal believers in central Hainan numbered nearly 10,000, but numbers decreased sharply when the churches were closed in the 1960s."[13]

Despite the horrific social upheavals and chaos during the Cultural Revolution, many faithful Kim Mun families continued to believe in Jesus Christ. In the early 1980s, when the hostile religious atmosphere in China began to thaw, many small fellowships of Kim Mun believers decided to register with the Three-Self Patriotic Movement (TSPM) in the hope they would be allowed to worship freely.

Several churches were established, with meetings typically held in thatched-roof huts. The Kim Mun believers in Yanyuan built a new church building, and 81 of the 93 households in Yanyuan joined the congregation.

In 1985, when a delegation of TSPM officials visited Enyuan village, situated on the side of a mountain, they reported, "The church has been built out of reeds and straw by the believers themselves. More than 80 Kim Mun believers met us, many in native costume."[14]

Despite encouraging signs and reports of hundreds of Kim Mun people still professing faith in Jesus Christ, several visitors to their churches had revealed alarming traits. In 1988, the editor of a Christian magazine visited Hainan and described the disturbing state of the Kim Mun churches he encountered:

> Most Christians are illiterate, so few have much knowledge of the Bible. The traditions of spiritual dancing and exorcism are attractive to them because they are visible and concrete manifestations of spiritual belief. Many older Christians consider reading the

Kim Mun Christians outside their chapel at Yanyuan
Bridge

Bible or hearing a sermon to be too abstract. On the other hand, younger Christians, more exposed to the outside world, find it difficult to express their belief in the same manner as their parents. These are some of the cultural realities, changes, and challenges that face the church in the Kim Mun districts of Hainan Island.[15]

Today, there remains a core of Kim Mun Christians in central Hainan, although the fellowships are fragmented, and recent visitors have found many believers still struggle with the heretical teachings that were handed down to them from previous generations.

Lamentably, more than a century after the first Kim Mun people believed in Jesus Christ, and despite the fact more than half a million members of this tribe are found scattered across south China, Vietnam, and Laos, not a single page of the Bible has ever been translated into Kim Mun to the present day, although various video and audio Gospel resources exist in their language.

The opening ceremony of a TSPM church for Kim Mun believers in 1985
Bridge

1940s and 1950s

Students at the Pitkin Presbyterian Girls' School in Hainan

The Hainan church amid social chaos

As the Second World War raged across Europe and Asia, a little-known historical event almost occurred in Hainan. The Nationalist government, led by the professing Christian Chiang Kai-shek (Mandarin name: Jiang Jieshi), made plans to set aside part of Hainan Island to be used to resettle Jewish refugees from Europe. As the initiative was unfolding, however, the invasion of the island by the Japanese caused the cancellation of the plan.[1]

Since the mid-1920s, Evangelical work in Hainan had become progressively more difficult due to the unstable social and political environment. Lawlessness flourished as bloodthirsty bandits roamed the countryside, terrorizing the population. The small pockets of Christians scattered throughout the island were left as sheep without a shepherd. Travel restrictions made visiting the believers dangerous and in many cases impossible.

In March 1950, Hainan Island was "liberated" by the Communists, becoming the final part of China to join the People's Republic. Soon after, the Hainan church entered a hibernation period which lasted for 30 years. During that time, little overt evangelism occurred as Christians were driven underground by the excessive anti-religion purges of the 1950s, 1960s and 1970s. Quietly, however, in one-to-one conversations between friends and family members, the gospel continued to spread.

In Haikou alone, the Evangelical churches contained more than 700 members in the years preceding the Communist take-over, and church leaders who had served so faithfully on the island for many years were deeply concerned about the plight of their flocks, as fierce Communist wolves encircled them.

The few remaining missionaries were forced to endure two and a half years under house arrest before being allowed to leave the country. The last foreign missionary was expelled from Hainan in 1952.

Hainan Christians who enjoyed close associations with the missionaries found themselves in deep trouble with the new atheist leaders of China. One of them, the principal of the Pitkin Presbyterian Girls' School, was sent to prison on the mainland, where she subsequently died.

Despite the overwhelming challenges, many Hainan Christians soldiered on through these dark times, clinging to Jesus Christ and cultivating their spiritual fellowship with God by depending on Him alone. The waves of persecution completely stripped the Hainan church of all foreign props and connections, forcing them to rely only on the power of the Holy Spirit for their survival and spiritual sustenance.

Margaret Moninger

Margaret Moninger was born in Iowa in 1891. After becoming a high school teacher, she applied to serve with the Presbyterian Mission. She arrived in Hainan in 1915, and just two days later she came face-to-face with the reality of life on the island when she accompanied missionary-doctor J. Franklin Kelly and his wife on a trip to Qionghai. As they approached a village riding in sedan chairs,

> squatters arose and blocked the road, holding out deformed hands and begging with scowling faces. As we came up they drew back, saying, "It's the doctor and his wife," and smiles appeared, as Dr. and Mrs. Kelly worked faithfully in the leper village near Qionghai. By long established custom, lepers could come out and beg on the first and fifteenth of the lunar months.[2]

As many newly-arrived missionaries do in the early part of their careers, Margaret wrote home about certain Hainan gastronomical customs that caught her attention. On one occasion, she encountered a man who was

> skinning a big rat. As the Chinese do not normally eat rats in this section of the country, I asked why. He said he was fixing it for his grandchildren to roast over the fire and eat so they wouldn't have boils! And then the small boys skewered it with pieces of bamboo and did roast it and I saw the youngest grandson, four or five years old, devouring his share with great delight a little later.[3]

After enjoying an initial "honeymoon period" that many new missionaries experience, difficulties began to emerge for Margaret. Her eyesight started to falter, which a doctor put down to the humid climate and her learning to read Chinese characters up and down the page instead of side to side as she was accustomed to reading.

In response to her eyestrain, Moninger abandoned reading and writing, and focused instead on learning Chinese just by speaking the language. Things improved immediately, and she astonished her colleagues by scoring 91 percent on her oral exam. Each missionary was required to send a formal progress report to the Presbyterian headquarters in New York, and Margaret surprised the board by submitting her first report in poetry! In part she wrote,

> Tis sad but true, my eyes went bad,
> And study's fate on the doctors hung;
> But after counsel grave and sad
> I've worked among with lungs and tongue.[4]

Margaret Moninger in 1942, aged 51

Margaret's rapid progress in obtaining a working knowledge of spoken Chinese prompted the Mission to change their policy for all new China recruits, who were now required to speak the language first before attempting to study Chinese characters.

In February 1917, Margaret met her first person from the Kim Mun tribe, and she immediately fell in love with this unpretentious, childlike people group. She excitedly wrote home, "We feel that we are having wonderful opportunities for the spread of the gospel here, with the Li first, and now the Kim Mun, literally begging for the message."[5]

Moninger's fascination with the Kim Mun, however, did not blind her to the fact that something foul was occurring among professing Christians in this tribe. She wrote, "Some of the people seem to have demon possession. They have very peculiar customs and they have learned a little of Christianity, and have a most peculiar mixture of it and paganism."[6]

Efforts to correct the slide into error of the Kim Mun churches occupied much of the missionaries' time from that point on, as they strove to remove the weeds before they choked the true faith. On one trip to the Kim Mun in 1918, Margaret reported, "About 100 people attended chapel every morning and the missionaries spend the day and night teaching the people about Christianity."[7]

In addition to her passion to reach the Li and Kim Mun minority groups in the interior of Hainan, over the course of her long and distinguished career, Margaret Moninger served as the principal of the Presbyterian schools at Qionghai, Nada, and Qiongzhong.

In the early twentieth century, Hainan was still considered an isolated outpost of Chinese civilization, and the difficult conditions required missionaries to be tough as they tilled the ground and sowed the seed of God's Word. While Margaret often found life difficult on the island, she was never slow at standing up to bullies when necessary. She was especially protective of the young girls who had been placed in her care.

In 1918, a battalion of Cantonese troops invaded the island. When she saw the soldiers enter the school compound, Margaret informed them politely but firmly, "This is a girls' school where no men are allowed!" She commented, "It's funny how ten or a dozen big fellows with their guns move when I speak."[8]

Later, during the Japanese military occupation of Hainan, Moninger was forbidden to leave her home in Nada for 15 months between 1937 and 1939. Those years were highly stressful for Margaret, and her health began to deteriorate after bouts with malaria had weakened her immune system. While she was confined in Nada, the Japanese troops brought chaos to the area, and 1,000 refugees flooded into the town to escape the carnage.

Finally, in 1941, Margaret was placed under house arrest by the Japanese, who repatriated her and her colleague Alice Skinner to the United States the following year. A touching scene unfolded on the morning they were expelled from Hainan. The Japanese allowed Skinner's maid to come and cook a farewell breakfast for the beloved departing missionaries. Margaret wrote,

> She scrambled eggs for us…wiping away her tears as she did so, and made the coffee. I stepped out into the kitchen for something, and when she saw me she dropped her egg spoon. She turned around and took me by the shoulders, almost shaking me in the excess of her emotion.[9]

After nearly three decades of exciting and stressful service on Hainan Island, Margaret Moninger peacefully slipped into eternity on March 21, 1950. Her adventures with Jesus had taken her to the other side of the world and back, and she died just a few miles from the home in Iowa where she had been born 58 years earlier.

Moninger's biography, *Educating the Women of Hainan*, was published nearly half a century after her death. A summary of the various roles she performed stated,

> She headed a girls' mission school, wrote scholarly articles on the Miao [Kim Mun] aborigines, collected botanical specimens for scientists at home, and served as mission treasurer. She was responsible for communications with American diplomatic personnel and was one of only six women appointed to the Presbyterian China Council, which set mission policy for all of China.[10]

A hungry rat helps lead a man to Christ

Despite the hardships being experienced by Christians in Hainan and throughout China, unique evidence of God at work encouraged His people, as the Holy Spirit continued to draw people to the cross during the 1940s and 1950s.

In one town, an old man with a cane was walking down the street, and as he passed a chapel he saw a large rat scampering through the gate, dragging a piece of paper that it had torn off a poster on the church wall. The man raised his cane to kill the rodent, but it darted into the safety of a drain, leaving the paper at the man's feet.

He picked it up, and read the words on it, which said, "Christ Jesus came into the world to save sinners, of whom I am chief" (1 Tim. 1:15).

The old man thought the incident was strange. He considered himself the worst of sinners, but he had no idea who Christ Jesus was. He looked up at the chapel and thought, "Perhaps this man lives here," and he entered the courtyard.

A Christian grandmother named Dong had just finished cleaning the chapel after a meeting, when the inquirer approached her.

"Does Christ Jesus live in this place?" he asked.

"Please come in, and we will tell you all about Him," she answered.

Then she led the old man into her guestroom and poured him a cup of tea. Granny Dong and her husband explained to their visitor who Christ Jesus is, and how He had come into the world to save sinners.

Before they had finished talking, the old man believed that the Lord would save him from his sins too, and he felt so happy when Mr. Dong prayed for him.

The strip of paper torn from the chapel wall did more good than if the rat had used it to line his bed, after all.[11]

God's repair job

Being a coastal province in the tropics, Hainan receives some of the most severe storms of any place in China, with typhoons rolling in from the South China Sea between May and October each year.

An impoverished widow in her 70s had recently surrendered her life to Jesus Christ, and she was growing daily in grace and the knowledge of God. Although she didn't understand many of the subtleties of her new faith, she knew that God loved her and cared about every detail of her life. She could call out to Him for any need, and He would not turn her away.

The widow's son was upset when he heard his mother had become a Christian, and he tried to persuade her to renounce the foreign religion and go back to burning incense in the temple.

Her home was a tiny one-room hut covered by straw thatch, and it was badly in need of repairs. Each time it rained, water came pouring through the gaps in the thatch and the hut shook from the wind because of a broken beam that was barely able to hold up the structure.

One day, fishermen knew a strong typhoon was approaching, and they raced around the town warning people to prepare. The widow's son rushed over to his mother's house and said,

"Mother, burn incense to the idols or tonight the house will be destroyed."

But she knew a better way, and kneeling down she prayed, "Father, you know I am a poor widow and have no money to call a carpenter to mend that beam, and I have no way of getting new straw to patch the roof either. Please look after my little house."

While still on her knees, the rain fell in bucketfuls and a whirlwind shook the little house violently. The son was terrified and shouted, "Mother, get up and burn incense! Get up quickly and burn incense!" but she continued, "Heavenly Father, you know all about the loose beam and my poor roof. You look after it, please."

After the worst of the typhoon had ceased, she rose from her knees and looked up to find that the violent shaking had brought the ends of the two beams tightly into place again! "Thank you, Heavenly Father," she said. "You knew all about it, and so you just mended it."

All that night the rain continued, but not a drop came through the thatched roof. Early the next morning the old woman went out to investigate. To her joy and amazement, she saw patches of new straw on the roof. The wind had blown it onto her roof from her neighbors' stacks, and the heavy rain had patted it into the holes as if a human hand had done the work! "Thank you, Heavenly Father," again and again she said. "You knew all about it, and so you just blew the straw over and mended it for me."[12]

Faithful believers in Nada

The church at Nada had been established in 1914. Later, a devout local believer Deng Weiqing donated a piece of land which remains the site of the Nada church to this day. A building large enough to seat 1,000 worshippers was constructed prior to the Communist takeover.

The pastor of the Nada church was a Hakka man named Yu Guanqiu, who had given his life to Jesus Christ in 1937 at the age of 19. After studying theology at the Chongqing Theological Seminary, he was assigned to shepherd the flock in Nada in 1948.

In the mid-1950s, the Nada church building was seized by the Communist Party and used as offices for the local Bureau of Light and Water. Refusing to be intimidated, the believers in Nada boldly constructed a small chapel directly across the street from the confiscated church, and they continued their services under Yu's leadership.

Yu was threatened many times by the authorities, but it seemed that each time the church was instructed to stop their meetings, more people came. As many as 1,000 people attended

Sister Baowen, Dr. Wang, and Pastor Yu Guanqiu in the late 1980s
Bridge

the Christmas services each year, crammed inside and outside the small chapel. In June 1963, the government could no longer stand the provocation. They arrested Yu and imprisoned him for seven years because of his unwavering dedication to Jesus Christ.

Yu was released from prison in 1970, and a decade later, in September 1980, he recommenced meetings in his home. Once again people came to sit under the teaching of this faithful shepherd.

In 1986, the government decided to hand back the large Nada church building, on the condition that Yu and his congregation would register with the Three-Self Patriotic Movement. Yu was criticized by some house church Christians for his decision to register. Yu, for his part, continued to preach the gospel and refused to abandon the flock that God had called him to shepherd.

For several years all seemed peaceful in the Nada church. Then suddenly, on July 4, 1993, Pastor Yu was forcibly removed as the church leader by the Hainan Religious Affairs Bureau. During the Sunday morning service, government officials seized the pulpit and told the stunned congregation that Yu and all the church staff had been fired.

It was announced that from that moment on the government would oversee the day-to-day operations of the church, and they alone would appoint speakers for all meetings. Yu tried to legally fight his dismissal, but his efforts were to no avail. In the eyes of the Communist authorities and their religious arm, Pastor Yu for years had refused to bow to their demands.

For many more years this man of God continued to minister from his home. Many people flocked to him for advice and counsel, but he would never again stand behind the pulpit of the church he had served for decades.

Sister Baowen's tribulation

Pastor Yu's sister, Baowen, was a qualified nurse who had kept the Nada Hospital open during the war after the Japanese arrested many of the medical staff. Because of her contact with foreign doctors and nurses, Baowen was falsely accused of being a spy for the West and was imprisoned for 20 years.

Prison was not a wasteful experience for Baowen, however. God's mercy and grace shone through the iron bars into her heart. During her long incarceration, Baowen met and married Liang Hanbin, who later became a faithful Bible teacher in the Nada church.

Prior to her arrest, Baowen had adopted a homeless orphan girl named Ling'en, who had a harelip disability. She deeply loved her new mother, and during Baowen's imprisonment, little

A house church meeting in Sister Baowen's home in the late 1980s
Bridge

Ling'en was often able to slip past the prison guards unnoticed to bring food and drink to her and other prisoners. Ling'en grew up to be a dedicated Christian and had three beautiful children of her own.

After she was finally released from prison, Baowen did not dwell on her difficulties, but looked forward to a bright future with the Lord. She continued her ministry and medical work in Nada and viewed the 20 years she spent behind bars as the crowning glory of her walk with Jesus.

In the late 1980s Baowen received a written apology from the prison authorities who had taken 20 years of her life. She gladly forgave them.

Ling'en (front right) with her family. Baowen and her husband are behind (center)
Bridge

1960s and 1970s

A Chinese work unit during the Cultural Revolution

A voice in the storm

For centuries Hainan was a place of exile where criminals were dispatched, and even during the 1960s and 1970s many people were sent to the island from the mainland. Among the exiles were Christians who had been arrested in other parts of China and sent to perform manual labor on the island.

One young man was taken from his home and sent to Hainan. He had been raised in a strong Christian family but had never found the courage to be a bold witness for the Living God. In Hainan, the young man was housed in a wooden dormitory along with many other laborers.

One day, months after his arrival, a typhoon began to stir in the South China Sea and winds of up to 200 miles per hour

(324 km/h) whipped across the island. The young man curled up on his bunk, content that the safest place was inside the dormitory and under his blanket. As the storm reached its full force, suddenly,

> he heard his name called. At first, he ignored it. The calling was persistent and seemed to come from outside. Perhaps, he thought, someone was in difficulty and needed him. Hurriedly dressing, he pulled a raincoat over his clothes and reluctantly stepped out into the fury of the storm, and he searched in the blinding rain for the person calling for him.
>
> As he searched, he heard a thundering crash like the sound of many trees cracking and falling. Finding no one, he turned to go back inside the dormitory, only there was just a pile of rubble and the groans of the injured. Most of his bunkmates were dead, crushed to death as the building collapsed.[1]

The voice in the storm and God's miraculous deliverance proved to be a life-changing event in the young man's life. It was said, "After discovering that God knew his name, the young man had a boldness in witnessing that he had never had before. More than 200 young people came to Christ in 18 months' time because of his experience of God's protection."[2]

The Chang family's great struggle

After the Communists finally assumed control of Hainan in 1951, the fledgling Christian community on the island braced themselves for hardship and suffering. For the first several years, however, things appeared relatively calm, as the Communist Party systematically gathered information and took stock of people, marking those they would target for punishment when the order was given.

For one Christian family, the dam suddenly burst one morning in 1959, when a respected believer, Brother Chang, said goodbye to his family and went off to work, oblivious to the fact that for almost 20 years he would not see them again. Indeed, for the next 15 years Chang's family didn't even know if he was dead or alive.

The authorities turned up at Chang's workplace and took him to be interrogated. As he was led away, he called out to his coworkers, "Don't be afraid. This is not the last judgment. We know that the last judgment will be in the presence of God."[3]

The Communist interrogators accused Chang of being a counter-revolutionary and a rightist, because he had refused to join the Three-Self Patriotic Movement. Chang denied the charges, and for the next year he underwent daily beatings and brainwashing sessions, as the government tried to force his faith from him and turn him into one of them.

Seeing that force would not break him, the authorities changed tactics and made false charges against Brother Chang. In the end he was convicted and sent to a prison labor camp, but he was not allowed to inform his family of the sentence.

As the days turned into weeks and months, Chang realized he was likely to be incarcerated for a long time. He recalled that John Bunyan, the author of *Pilgrim's Progress*, had been imprisoned 20 years for his faith, and he determined two things in his heart. First, he would not deny the Lord Jesus Christ, no matter what pressure was exerted against him, and second, he wanted to witness for the Lord by being a model prisoner.

Over time, the prison guards saw that Chang was different from the other inmates. He always had a positive attitude, even after being beaten, and he sometimes even smiled at them. Many years later, when he was released, the prison director told Chang's family, "Many who have passed through here we do not know. This man we know thoroughly. He is completely honorable and trustworthy."[4]

The most difficult thing for both Chang and his family was the total lack of communication. For 15 years they had no clue where he was being held or if he was still alive. In 1974 he fell gravely ill, causing his head to swell to almost double its normal size. Chang was told by a prison guard that he should write a letter to his family and ask them to bring nutritious food to the prison for him, or he would soon die.

When his family received the letter, they were overjoyed to know that Chang was still alive. Despite their own extreme poverty they rallied to his aid, with his son making repeated long journeys to the labor camp to take supplies to him. One day the prison authorities asked Chang,

> "Why is your family so different? They're not like the others!" He then shared his Christian faith with them. He was able to witness for Christ during those long years of incarceration. When at last he was being released, the authorities asked him, "If we held you for 30 years would you still believe in Jesus?" He replied, "I would believe more strongly than ever."[5]

Only later did Brother Chang discover that his wife and children had been forced to endure even worse trials during the years he was in prison. Not only did they suffer from not knowing what had happened to him, but they had been denied access to government food coupons and had struggled to survive. As family members of a counter-revolutionary, they were blocked from gaining employment and the children were barred from receiving any kind of education.

Finally, the Chang family was reunited, and they continued to serve Christ together. Over time, the Lord healed many of the physical and emotional scars they carried, and their testimony of God's faithfulness was a tremendous encouragement to other Christians. Years later, a mission publication that interviewed Brother Chang remarked,

> The Christian courage, the fortitude, and the example of this one family should be enough to make all of us assess our relationship

to Jesus Christ. It should remove all cause for grumbling and complaining, and renew a determination within us to stand and be counted as children of the Lord.... The gospel of the kingdom not only transforms lives and keeps them in the most difficult of circumstances. Pastor Chang and his family are twentieth-century saints who verify God's sufficiency in every area of life.[6]

Blessings at Wanning

Wanning, on the east coast of Hainan, has long been considered a key center for Christianity on the island, with several thriving churches in the area prior to the advent of Communism in 1949. Throughout the 1970s, Hong Kong Christians frequently visited Wanning, reporting on the state of the churches as they sought to bounce back from the decades of Mao's draconian rule. After one visit in the late 1970s, a Hong Kong believer wrote,

> I am anxious to tell you of my experiences during my visit to Hainan. The Lichi Commune in Wanning County is the place where Christians are most active in eastern Hainan. In that area there were churches even before liberation. Believers were able to conduct normal Christian life until the Cultural Revolution, when churches were destroyed and Christians could not carry on their usual activities.
>
> During the past two or three years, believers have been able to conduct semi-open Christian activities. More recently believers have been meeting openly. They usually meet every Saturday and Sunday evening....
>
> The content of their testimonies usually includes thanksgiving for having been called into the kingdom of God, explanation of how they led others to the Lord, and testimony of how the power of the Holy Spirit made them able to heal the sick. Earnest believers in that area erected a spiritual hospital in the name of the Lord and healed many by His Name. It has been very effective, and many have been led to the Lord through healing....

The number of people gathering in these house church meetings is several dozen, and sometimes it reaches over 100. They divide their meeting places into several spots, each at the home of a certain believer. In Wanning County alone, the number of Christians reaches several thousand.[7]

By 2002, the Three-Self churches in Wanning reported 10,800 members meeting in 34 churches throughout the county,[8] while one researcher noted, "Wanning may have 10,000 believers, 90 percent of whom meet in independent house churches."[9]

The rich spiritual legacy established in Wanning many decades ago has continued to the present time. Today, the county has one of the highest concentrations of Christians in Hainan, with an estimated 65,000 Evangelical Christians meeting in both registered churches and house church fellowships throughout Wanning.[10] This figure represents approximately 11.5 percent of the population of the county.

The Great Physician makes a house call

As the 1970s drew to a close, three decades of terror and stress for the body of Christ in Hainan was beginning to dissipate. Over time, those who had survived the fierce onslaught realized that not only had God caused them to remain in the faith, but He had performed a great miracle. All over the island and throughout China, news emerged of an increased number of believers, packed church meetings, and a population that had been so stripped of inner reality by the Communists that millions of people were now wide open to the claims of the gospel.

Just one of many testimonies to emerge in Hainan told of the grace and power of Jesus Christ. An elderly Christian doctor, Wang, had been trained in Western medicine. Because of that foreign connection, the Communist Party saw him as a threat, and they especially despised him because he was an elder of the church in Nada.

In the 1960s, when people were starving during a severe famine brought on by Mao's foolish policies, Wang continued to treat people. Money was scarce, however, so often his only payment was a few white turnips or some eggs tied in a dingy cloth, for that was all the people could afford.

When the Cultural Revolution commenced in 1966, Wang was immediately persecuted. He was paraded through the streets by merciless Red Guards, with jeering people hurling abuse at him, including some of his neighbors who had benefitted from his medical treatment.

In prison, Dr. Wang was brutally beaten for being a Christian. He suffered a permanent injury, although he always refused to talk about the incident that caused it. Wang was told he would never be able to walk again, and after gaining his release, he was confined to his bed in a small upstairs room, where his family cared for him.

One night, after the rest of his family had gone to sleep, the wife of Wang's eldest son heard the creaking sound of the great wooden gate open in the courtyard. Jumping out of bed,

> she ran out on the narrow veranda and looked down just as a white-clad figure entered the house. Could it be a thief? Barefooted, she slipped down the steep stairway and peered cautiously into each room below. No one was there except family members who were sound asleep.
>
> Meanwhile, in the little room upstairs, old Dr. Wang stirred in his sleep. Suddenly a shimmering light shone down upon him, and his eyes opened to a miraculous vision of the Lord Jesus Christ standing beside his bed. "Son," he heard Jesus say, "Get up and walk!"

"I can't," he replied, overwhelmed with surprise and wonder. "I cannot walk." So, Jesus reached out His hands and helped him sit up.

Without hesitation the old man obeyed. He rose from his bed and began walking. The Lord Jesus Himself had touched him. Then Dr. Wang began to laugh aloud with joy. It was 2:20 in the morning.[11]

Other family members, who had been fast asleep, heard the laughter and they raced to see what was happening. They found Wang walking around laughing and thought he had lost his mind. When they took hold of his arms to prevent him from falling, Wang firmly said,

"Keep your hands off me! I am not out of my mind. The Lord Jesus came to this room! He healed me!"

Then, to prove his words, he walked down the steep stairway from his room to the ground floor below. There he turned around, smiled at his frightened family, and began walking up again, taking steady, even steps. The joy of the family knew no bounds....

It was the middle of the night, but the news could not wait until morning. The entire family trooped over to the second son's home on another street. "Look! Grandpa is walking!" cried a young grandson, and one by one the startled relatives joined the excited group. Laughing and rejoicing, they gave thanks to God together.[12]

On the following Sunday, the house church where believers gathered was overflowing with people who crowded into every room. Dozens more stood outside in the courtyard trying to peer in through the windows. When Dr. Wang began to speak, a hush fell over the crowd. After he shared what had happened, questions began to flow, which he answered one by one:

"Yes, my eyes were open when I saw the Lord Jesus…. Yes, His face was full of love…. His face seemed to shine."

Dr. Wang now travels far and wide on his bicycle, telling all who will listen about the power of Jesus. And people are not only listening, but they are also calling on the Name of the Lord and being saved![13]

Like the first signs of spring after a long and bitter winter, the church in Hainan slowly responded to the sun's rays in the late 1970s. Mao Zedong had died in 1976 and the Gang of Four had been overthrown. Winds of change were in the air across the island and throughout China. Cautiously, one step at a time, the body of Christ began to resurface. They had learned that God would never forsake them, and that He had been quietly at work all those years, preserving His inheritance and causing the Name of Jesus to be exalted.

As the 1970s came to an end, the scene was set for a remarkable period, when the seed that had been buried underground for three decades would spring to life and produce a mighty harvest for the kingdom of God in Hainan.

The Indonesians

Two young Indonesian men return from a successful hunt
Paul Hattaway

Deceived by promises of a Communist utopia

Although few people realize it, approximately 6,000 Indonesians live in central Hainan Island's Qionghai County.

Between 1960 and 1967 the Communist authorities in China issued an invitation to ethnic-Chinese in Indonesia to "return to the Motherland." The Indonesian government at the time was terrified by the spread of Communism throughout Southeast Asia, and many thousands of suspected Communist sympathizers were rounded up and executed. Chinese people were chief among the suspects, and great hardships were endured by Chinese throughout Indonesia.

In that environment, the offer of migrating away from Indonesia appealed to many terrorized families, and thousands of people made their way north to Mao Zedong's China.

Attracted by China's promise of free land and a vibrant new society with freedom of speech and religion, the Indonesians of Chinese descent who agreed to move to Hainan soon found the reality to be starkly different. Most of them were resettled in the large Xinglong Overseas Chinese Farm, which had formerly been used as a prison labor camp and was set amid a thick, impenetrable forest. The Communist utopia they had been promised proved to be more like a slave camp or a prison.

Ironically, most of the Indonesians who made the journey to Hainan were not ethnic-Han Chinese at all, but tribal people from the Toraja region on the Indonesian island of Sulawesi. Although Sulawesi contains a rich and diverse collection of tribes and is home to 144 distinct Malayo-Polynesian languages, the families who came to Hainan decided to speak standard Indonesian to communicate with each other. The tribal immigrants, however, still called themselves Oran Toraja, meaning "people from Toraja."

In a surprise to the Chinese Communist Party, approximately half of the Indonesians who settled in Hainan were Christians. Their faith gave them hope, but when they were forbidden to worship in the 1960s and their leaders were harshly persecuted, many wished they had never taken up the offer of a new life in China.

The Indonesians faced extreme hardships when they first arrived in Hainan. Back in Sulawesi they led peaceful and relaxed lives, but in Hainan they had to work hard just to survive, with one source noting, "Many of the new arrivals broke down in tears.... They were not farmers; they had to learn how to plant crops and reap harvests."[1]

Sad letters from a strange land

Indonesians continued to migrate to Hainan throughout the 1960s and beyond, but the hardships they faced caused many to return home if they were able to. Occasionally, letters from struggling Indonesians appeared in various publications outside China, including the following laments from four newly-arrived Indonesian Christians:

> *"Dear beloved brothers and sisters in Christ. Grace and peace from God our Father and our Lord Jesus Christ. I've just arrived from Indonesia, but there is no place here to worship God and glorify His Name. My spiritual life is now very weak. Pray there may be a plan for us to return to where there is a church that preaches the Gospel of Christ's precious Blood, and that men may be delivered from death to life, so that we may again see God's care for us.... This is my hope. Emmanuel."[2]*

> *"Dear Pastor: I failed my entrance exam to the university here because I am not sufficiently 'progressive' and I still have religious thoughts. Now I know you were right to warn me not to come to China, but I cannot leave."[3]*

> *"It is now almost four years since I left Indonesia.... Those who have come to this land have greatly changed. Some have even turned their backs on the Lord and His truth. This causes me deep grief.*

But there is a small group among our ranks who are still strong and brave for the Lord and continue to walk with Him. Because of their faith they are triumphant....

I can pray and read the Bible each day and I sometimes attend church. I am gladly and willingly walking the Calvary Road and bearing my cross for Him. It is only this kind of life which is fully satisfying and is not in vain. I also thank God for His power and protection in keeping me from joining the Communist Youth Corps. I know His reason for this, for if I had joined it would have meant that I would need to publicly deny my Lord before others."[4]

"I have been a believer since 1942. In Indonesia the church was nearby and I often met with our pastor. In the 1960s I had to return to China, but we were not allowed to bring our Bibles or hymnals with us. I became a lost sheep, daily longing for God to visit His people.... Recently several overseas Chinese have joined us, but they too arrived without Bibles. Can you help us with spiritual food?"[5]

Gradually, after much sweat and heartache, the Indonesians began to eke out a living from the Hainan soil. They finally won their struggle for survival, and the land produced good yields of coffee, pepper, coconut, and rubber.

While Indonesians were struggling to come to terms with life in Hainan, the Chinese Communist authorities were increasingly spreading their influence among churches in Indonesia in the hope that they could gain control of that key Southeast Asian nation. An Indonesian pastor said in 1954,

Communism is the greatest problem facing the Christian Church in Indonesia. The Communists now are working to separate Christians from the Church. They have succeeded in weaning from the Sunday school about 40 percent of non-Christian Chinese children who formerly attended…. The propaganda of the Communists makes young people feel that they are unpatriotic Chinese unless they are for Communism.[6]

The first churches

For years the remnant of Indonesian Christians in Hainan had no building to worship in and no church leaders. Despite the trials of living through Mao's Cultural Revolution from 1966 to 1976, the Indonesians "were still able to maintain a personal and ethnic identity. Those who believed in Jesus Christ had been allowed to meet, but as soon as the Cultural Revolution broke out, Christian worship was banned, and believers were doubly persecuted."[7]

Although small groups of Christians had met in homes during the 1960s and 1970s, the first Indonesian Three-Self church in Hainan was established in October 1989. It was named the Gereja Batania (Church of Bethany). At the opening dedication service, Christians from the nearby Kim Mun tribe joined visitors from Hong Kong and Indonesia as the 250-seat chapel was filled to overflowing.

The congregation of the main Indonesian church in Hainan in 1989
Bridge

The Indonesians today

Today, the majority of Indonesians in Hainan are dedicated Christians. They worship in several registered churches as well as many unregistered meetings. After the Gereja Batania opened, the church's seating capacity of 300 immediately proved too small as crowds flocked to the meetings.

In May 1992, the second registered Indonesian church in Hainan, the Gereja Injili Kemah Pertemuan (Church of the Tabernacle), was dedicated in Ding'an County. Most of the 90,000 Yuan ($18,000) construction cost for the 250-seat chapel was raised by Christians in Indonesia. Chinese and Kim Mun believers also use the building for services at different times.

Since the mid-1980s, church leaders from their homeland of Toraja have regularly traveled to Hainan to encourage and train the Indonesian believers in the Word of God.

Hainan's Indonesian Christians continue to meet three or four times each week and they love to sing to the Lord. Like birds that were caged for a long time, they now relish their freedom, and they thank God for helping them overcome the extreme difficulties they have encountered during their brief history on Hainan Island.[8]

1980s

A decade of harvest

During the brutal decade of the Cultural Revolution (1966 to 1976), Hainan's Christians continued to meet secretly in small groups, while all official church activities ceased for a 15-year period from 1966 to 1981. Some believers had to hide their faith not only from the authorities but also from some of the corrupt men who managed to position themselves as leaders of the Three-Self Church.

In 1981, five years after Mao Zedong's death, a small group of Christians gathered in Haikou and asked the authorities to permit them to legally worship again. Two years later the former Haikou church building at Yanzao was returned by the government and meetings recommenced. On March 31, 1985, three church workers were ordained by the TSPM in a ceremony witnessed by more than 400 believers.

As Christians throughout Hainan learned to fellowship together in the post-Mao era, it soon became apparent that God had supernaturally intervened to help His children come through the fiery furnace of affliction. One letter from a believer in 1982 said,

> Since the beginning of the 1980s when we began to gather as believers, more and more people have come to believe in the Lord. At that time, we only had 70 Christians and we came to the Lord with our illnesses and problems. God has healed all our illnesses, and everyone has tasted of the goodness of the Lord. We all have the power and motivation to work among our relatives

and friends, witnessing for Jesus. Now we have more than 200 people at our meetings and we greatly need spiritual food.[1]

By 1987, churches throughout the island were overflowing with people. Many elderly believers reemerged into the light, their faith having been refined by years of harsh persecution. Veteran British missionary Leslie Lyall enthusiastically reported, "Hainan is an idolatrous place, but even here the church is growing apace, despite persecution during the 1950s and 1960s when many pastors were murdered. Today, Christians are found all over the island, meeting in many house fellowships."[2]

When one house church leader in Hainan was asked how the flock under his care had grown so strongly without any outside influence, his honest response was, "Probably it is because we don't have pastors; we don't have missionaries; we don't have church buildings; and we don't have song books.... Therefore God, in His great mercy for us, often demonstrated His power among us to assure our weak faith."[3]

For much of the decade, true disciples of Jesus Christ in Hainan struggled to reconnect with one another, but small groups of believers gradually contacted each other and merged

The first meeting of Hainan Three-Self Church leaders in 1985
Bridge

into small networks, strengthening the body of Christ. Preachers, Bibles, and other resources were shared, and Christians who most needed help found relief.

The result was explosive growth, and a greater harvest of souls was reaped in a short period of time in Hainan than during all the years of the missionary era combined. Before that happened, however, many new believers had been unsure how to proceed in the faith. One teenage boy wrote from Hainan in 1985,

> There are so few Christians in our area. In our commune we are the only ones. In the whole county there is only a handful. When we want to attend worship services, we must walk 10 miles (16 km) to a town. The distance does not bother us. What disappoints us is that there is no real church or preacher to lead us.
>
> Believers here have a problem finding Christian spouses, but that will not deter me from following the Lord. My mind is made up to believe and follow Him. I want to ask you a question, but please don't laugh: What are the requirements for becoming a pastor? If you have some Bible study aids, please send me some. I will pay for them.[4]

Set free to serve

In the mid-1980s, a young house church evangelist, Sister Kan, traveled to Hainan to help pioneer house churches. Although she had little education and came from a rough family background, the Holy Spirit used her in a wonderful way to reach many people for Jesus Christ. This is part of her testimony:

> I am from a family of Communist Party members. We were all atheists. Nine years ago, after I graduated from middle school, I was sent to work in a rural village. It was a very superstitious place. One night while trying to sleep, several evil spirits came upon me. Next day, my personality was completely changed. I never smiled or laughed again. People thought I was mentally

ill, and I was sent to an institution in the city, where they put me on medication. I was sedated, but not cured....

Sometime later, my younger sister became a Christian. When she came home and told the family about Jesus, I went with her to a house church. I knew immediately that Jesus Christ was the true Savior. Soon afterwards, I was baptized....

I was still working in a factory, but whenever I had a free moment I went to the house church. The leaders gave me books to read and tapes to listen to. I spent a lot of time reading the Bible, and later the leaders asked me and another young Christian to start a house church....

I went to Hainan because I thought I needed a break, but it turned out to be a "Macedonian call." The island was a stronghold of demonic spirits. A younger sister came to be my ministry partner, and we spent much time in prayer.

About a year ago, we were urgently requested to go to a home where a man was demon-possessed. We didn't want to go, but the Holy Spirit told us to. When we got to the house, we found a lot of people and commotion. My younger partner, who is usually very soft-spoken, was filled with the Holy Spirit and commanded the people to be quiet. I led the demon-possessed man to the Lord. Then in Jesus' Name we bound the demons and laid hands on the man and cast them out. He was set free and testified to the power of Jesus. All the villagers recognized that Jesus is the most powerful God.

We often see God perform wonderful healings, but our biggest responsibility is to disciple the many new Christians. In a nearby village we are discipling more than 2,000 new believers.

My partner and I are still like infants, learning together. We spend much time waiting before the Lord, and the Holy Spirit constantly guides us. We sense the Lord leading us to go to another village for a period of pioneer evangelism.[5]

The revival experienced by these young women was typical of other movements to Christ in Hainan at the time, which resulted in explosive growth. When the respected Chinese church historian Jonathan Chao visited Hainan in 1987, he made these observations about the state of the churches on the island:

> Due to the lack of official, registered churches, most believers congregate in homes, with attendance normally numbering several hundred people. This causes severe overcrowding, which forces the worshippers to sit on mats on the ground. There is a need for microphones and loudspeakers for house churches that utilize many different rooms or which are in multi-storied dwellings.[6]

Registered churches bloom in Hainan

As the religious environment in China continued to relax during the 1980s, Three-Self congregations emerged in many parts of Hainan. Church buildings and chapels that had been confiscated in the 1950s and 1960s were returned by the government, although many were in a state of disrepair. Local Christians banded together to help with the renovation work, and when a delegation of China Christian Council officials toured the island in 1985, they oversaw the reopening of many churches. *Tianfeng* (the magazine of the TSPM) reported on their visit:

> In Danzhou we visited the large church there. More than 80 church workers and believers attended a tea party. The church has been restored and repaired, and every Sunday 300 to 400 Christians come to the service.
>
> Qiongzhong has many Li and Kim Mun people. Eleven churches have been reopened in this county, and there are also five meeting points....
>
> Changliushui village in Qiongzhong County has 150 inhabitants, all of whom are believers. There has never been any theft in the village and their reputation for good public order is known throughout the county....
>
> There are more than 3,000 Christians in Wanning County and many more people want to join the church.... It is encouraging to learn about the large numbers of Christians in Hainan.... Let

us pray that the gospel will continue to flourish on this tropical island.[7]

As China relaxed and opened its doors to the outside world during the 1980s, a small number of foreign Christians arrived on the island, eager to do good works and share Christ with people. Canadians Kevin and Julia Garratt arrived in the late 1980s to teach English at a university, but the course of their service soon took a dramatic shift when one of their fellow workers explained the terrible stench behind the Garratt's house.

Julia assumed the worker was referring to what she assumed had been the smell of decaying garbage. But the worker replied, "No, it is from unwanted babies. China's one child policy stresses that farmers need a son to work the farm and care for them in

The TSPM church at Fucheng, surrounded by high-rise apartments

their old age. Girls go to their husband's families after marriage, so when a girl is born, it's a hard decision...."[8]

The Garratts were shocked and appalled at the cheapness of human life, and cried out to God, asking Him to show them what they could do. He led them to the Scriptures, where they read, "You were thrown out into the open field, for on the day you were born you were despised. Then I passed by and saw you kicking about in your blood.... I said to you, 'Live!'" (Ezek. 16:5–6).

Convinced that Christ wanted those babies to live, the Garratts trusted God to provide the funds and place, and things gradually fell into place for them to establish a kindergarten and nursery school for abandoned children. They also adopted one of the little girls Hannah into their own family. Within two years the Garratts reported, "Hundreds of children lived! A full-scale children's home with 100 toddlers and a special needs center was operational.... The orphanage received a credential permitting adoptions, enabling many children to find their forever families."[9]

1990s

A packed Three-Self Church meeting
RCMI

A perfect storm

For centuries, the people of Hainan have been battered by regular typhoons that wreak havoc along the coast every year. When the 1990s commenced, Christianity in Hainan still only had a marginal presence, with less than one percent of the population professing to follow Jesus Christ. Although a smattering of believers was found around the island, few people had ever heard the gospel even once in their lives. When a foreign Christian arrived on the island to implement a humanitarian project in 1992, he was confronted by this revealing conversation with the local people:

I had come to work with the registered church pastor in the area of the province which had by far the most Christians, both house church and registered church Christians. The town only had two major roads. I checked into the local hostel and asked the people behind the counter where the church building was in the town.

They asked, "What's a church?"

I said, "A church is where Christians worship."

They replied, "What's a Christian?"

When I told them, "A Christian is a follower of Jesus." They asked, "Who is Jesus?"

The next group I asked had similar responses, but they decided that a Buddhist temple 12 miles (20 km) up the road must be what I was looking for. The next group informed me that there were no churches in the province. Between the first eight groups of people I asked, there were three who had no idea what I was talking about, three who decided it was the Buddhist temple, and two who said there were no churches in the province.[1]

God, who holds history in His hands and does as He pleases, was about to bring an unexpected and far-reaching revival to the church in Hainan—a heavenly visitation so powerful and sudden that many were caught by surprise. Even some long-term China-watchers were left dumbfounded, not knowing how it had unfolded.

In 1992, the authorities in Hainan surprised many people by announcing there were 37,000 Evangelical believers on the island, meeting in 21 registered churches and 41 meeting points.[2] Although this figure did not include any of the unregistered house church believers scattered throughout Hainan's towns and villages, it represented a huge increase from just 4,000 Evangelicals that had been published by the same official source just four years earlier in 1988.[3]

Although this apparent increase seems encouraging, the American missionary who lived in Hainan at the time disputes the claim. He said,

I personally visited every Three-Self church in Hainan during the 1990s, and I know for sure that there were not 37,000 members among all of them. At best, I estimate that no more than 2,000 people attended registered churches in any given week. I believe the number was a fabrication created by Li Xunru, the provincial leader of the Three-Self Patriotic Movement, who probably wanted to enhance his reputation and influence with the central government by claiming he was responsible for many more believers than was the case.[4]

Despite the tiny number of Christians in Hainan at the time, God looked down from heaven and decided He would glorify His Name among the millions of Hainanese who had never heard of Him. The Holy Spirit began to blow, whipping up a spiritual typhoon that was to strike the island with unprecedented fury.

Dragged from the pulpit

One catalyst for the explosive growth of the church in Hainan during the 1990s came from an unexpected source, with the actions of a wicked church leader causing disgust among many Christians. This ultimately proved instrumental in creating a hunger in the hearts of many believers to walk intimately with God and to make Him known to others.

Qionghai and Haikou were two cities in Hainan where believers experienced much persecution in the 1990s because of corrupt and wicked Three-Self Church leaders. Li Xunru, the provincial TSPM leader, hailed from Qionghai. From the early-to-mid 1990s he led a church in the city, but during the week he traveled to the capital Haikou where he worked in the combined offices of the Three-Self Church and the China Christian Council.

Li, who was the provincial head of these two organizations, was renowned for his intense hatred of the unregistered house churches in Hainan, but his demonic fury spilled over to such an extent that he even began to persecute the registered churches under his control.

On one occasion, an Indonesian believer named Wong Ping Tak came from Hong Kong and went through all the proper channels to speak at the Indonesian church in Wanning. Wong had planted three small churches among the Indonesians on previous visits to the island, all of which were officially registered with the government.

Li Xunru granted Wong permission to speak in the church and even hosted him in his home when he first arrived on the island. When Wong reached Wanning, however, Li had the Indonesian preacher arrested and put in prison because he had brought three or four Bibles with him that were printed in Hong Kong. Wong was charged with illegal literature distribution and was barred from entering Hainan again.

At the time, the two largest Three-Self churches in Hainan were blessed to have God-fearing pastors who loved Jesus Christ and endeavored to honor God's Word within the context of the government church. Because these pastors were genuine believers, Li continually pressured them to propagate Communist Party ideology.

Li Xunru considered the sermons of the pastor in Danzhou to be overly evangelistic, so he had him literally removed from the pulpit during a Sunday morning service. The faithful pastor was handcuffed and dragged away in front of his stunned congregation, and he was subsequently imprisoned for a long time. While he was languishing behind bars, Li had the pastor replaced by a preacher considered less of a threat to Li and the Communist Party.

In Haikou, a female Three-Self pastor named Chen was also removed during a worship service and placed under house arrest. Chen's troubles began when she wanted to send a co-worker to mainland China for theological training. Li Xunru refused to let the worker go and instead appointed two government employees—neither of whom were Christians—to attend the seminary.

In April 1993, Pastor Chen was handed a note before the start of a church service. It was from the United Workers Front director and said, "We will be videotaping the service today. Do not interfere." According to one report,

> As soon as the service started the doors were blocked, and Public Security Bureau employees began to go up and down every aisle taking close-ups of everyone in the congregation. Their purposes were three-fold: to establish a file of everyone involved in the church; to intimidate the believers; and to use the footage as false evidence of "foreign contact" against the pastor (two foreigners were present).[5]

Ironically, the efforts of corrupt government church leaders like Li Xunru did nothing to quell the plans of the Spirit of God, and their vile practices drove many real Christians away from the Three-Self churches.

Thousands of believers had been willing to obey the law and register via the proper channels, but the unreasonable demands placed on them by Three-Self officials caused them to become thoroughly disillusioned. Spurred into action by Li Xunru's disgraceful persecution of his own church leaders, the majority of Christians in Hainan decided to remain outside the control of the Three-Self Church, choosing to meet in unregistered house church meetings instead.

A Holy Spirit-inspired strategy

Although a small house church movement existed in Hainan throughout the 1980s, it lacked the organization and vision needed to impact a large proportion of the population. This all began to change in 1991, when a Baptist missionary and his family were used by God to launch a training program based on a fresh start that ignored the traditions and spiritual baggage of their home denominations in the West.

More than two decades later, years after he and his family had left China, the missionary released a series of videos, in which he shared what it was God had led him to implement in Hainan that helped launch a massive revival encompassing every section of Hainan society. In one message, the American missionary recalled an epiphany he had in which the Holy Spirit revealed God's strategy for effectively reaching the Hainanese people:

> My wife and I were serving among an unengaged people group of six-and-a-half million people. Their language had not been reduced to writing, so we couldn't go to language school to learn it. We had to just pick it up.
>
> I had a plan where I was going to start with two-year-olds and gradually talk with older and older people until I could talk with

A house church worship meeting
RCMI

adults. It seemed like a good plan to me, but early on I went to a village and couldn't see any children, but I went up to one really old lady who was 97-years-old. This woman had never heard of the terms "Jesus," "church," "Bible," or "Christian." She was as lost as a person can be.

As I got ready to leave the village I reached into my pocket and offered her a Chinese Gospel tract but she declined it, saying she couldn't read. She said her son couldn't read either, and in fact no one in the entire village could read. I suddenly felt very helpless. Clearly my language skills were not sufficient to share the gospel with this woman. There were no Christians I could refer her to or churches I could introduce her to. There was no Christian radio or television broadcasts in her language.

At first, I consoled myself with the thought that eventually I would learn the language and share the gospel with people. But then I realized that even if I led one person every day to the Lord from that point until I was old enough to retire, there would only be about 15,000 new converts, which wouldn't be a drop in the bucket for this group of well over six million people. It wouldn't even come close to keeping up with the population growth....

I also realized that it wasn't enough to have converts. We needed disciples, which meant we needed churches. I didn't know how this was possible, but hoped that maybe in our first five-year term I could lead enough people to the Lord and train them to be church-planting trainers. I thought that perhaps I could work with a group of 20 church-planting teams, and each of those teams could plant a church every year. Even if I was able to do that, I worked out that after 250 years, Hainan would still only have a modest number of churches among its millions of people. That wasn't going to work either.

Then I realized that if I could plant just one church, and that church would multiply every year— and each daughter church would also multiply every year—then the entire island could be reached in just 17 years.

That is what happened! In fact, it occurred faster than 17 years, and every village had a church. The turning point came when I decided to only focus on doing things that would result in making disciples that multiplied, and formed churches that multiplied. I realized that this strategy was the only way to get the job done.[6]

Explosive growth

After a New Testament pattern of Christianity was implemented in Hainan, similar explosive growth occurred on the island like how revival spread among the first Christians in the Book of Acts. As the movement gathered momentum at an astonishing rate, the missionary summarized the spectacular growth experienced by just one house church network in Hainan:

> Between April 1993 and April 1998, the number of believers related to this one network increased from fewer than 100 to 55,000, and the number of churches grew from just three to around 550. This means there was a church for every 20,000 people anywhere you looked on the island. That is, you could not find a geographical area with a population of 20,000 people or more that did not have a church. The work of evangelism and church planting was being entirely handled by local Christians by the end of this five-year period.[7]

The timing of this heaven-sent revival in Hainan coincided with the arrival of house church evangelists from mainland China—men and women who had been called by God to reach the people of China's southernmost province. For centuries, a place at the southern tip of the island had been known as Tianya Haijiao ("end of the earth") to describe the island's extreme isolation. The evangelists chose that very spot, in Sanya County, to begin their work because they wanted to obey Jesus' command to take the gospel to the ends of the earth!

In the history of great Christian revivals around the world, the outpouring of God's power upon a nation is usually preceded by the Holy Spirit preparing hearts for repentance, so that when the revival begins, people's hearts are often like dry tinder, and the spark of revival soon spreads into a raging fire that quickly touches tens or even hundreds of thousands of lives. That was the case in Hainan, where seemingly small efforts to share the gospel with people often produced a massive impact for the kingdom of God.

For example, a Hainanese Christian who lived in Hong Kong—where he served as a deacon in his local church—heard that something amazing seemed to be happening on his home island. He traveled there and was determined to hold a public evangelistic rally, without regard to the differences between Hong Kong and Communist China, where all such meetings were strictly forbidden. An eyewitness at the meeting reported,

> Amazingly he was not arrested, although there was some later political fall-out for some local officials, and one of his coworkers later had trouble getting into the province.
>
> The rally was held outdoors in the evening and there were around 1,000 people in attendance, which was a large proportion of the population of that town. At the conclusion of the rally an invitation to receive Jesus was given.
>
> Quite a few people raised their hands to indicate a decision for Christ. The speaker assumed that they hadn't understood, so he explained the gospel again in terms of the harshest discipleship required to be a follower of Christ. This time, he asked people to come forward and stand directly under the main light which was next to where he was speaking. It was fully dark by this time, so standing in the light meant that people would be clearly identified as a Christian in this very illegal context, which was almost certain to lead to government persecution.
>
> At first no one moved. It was so quiet you could hear a pin drop. Then, finally, a young man walked to the front and stood

beside the speaker. Slowly, by ones and twos, others joined him. In the end, 60 people accepted Christ as their Lord that evening. Despite the likelihood of immediate persecution, they were ready to boldly identify with Jesus Christ.[8]

Almost all Christians who shared their faith in Hainan during this extraordinary time of heavenly visitation found receptive hearts eager to embrace the gospel. Four American believers had traveled to Hainan on two-year English teaching jobs. They came with no intention of leading large numbers of people to the faith, but hoped they might be able to discreetly share their faith with a few students outside the classroom. In Hainan during the 1990s, however, the Lord Jesus Christ took their efforts and multiplied them supernaturally, as He once did with some loaves and fishes. A report said of the English teachers,

> They were able to lead a number of their students to the Lord and began to disciple them over the course of their time in China. Toward the end of their period of service, however, they started to worry about what would happen when they left to return to the United States. Some of the new converts had not been accepted into any house church, and the registered church was not supplying adequate teaching or support.
>
> The teachers decided to have a retreat. They rented a bus, filled it with students they had won to the Lord, and took off for the mountains, where they rented the wing of a hotel and held a spiritual retreat. They structured it in such a way that the students had meaningful interaction with each other during the week. They shared testimonies, worshipped together, were trained how to share their faith, and spent lots of time just enjoying informal fellowship.
>
> I was fortunate enough to attend this event. For me, the first evening was a highlight. These new believers played *Bible Trivia* together, and their Bible knowledge greatly impressed me. I think they only missed two questions during the whole game. It was an

encouragement for them to see other young people from the same background who were equally serious about their new faith.[9]

Because of the intentional focus on evangelism and discipleship, growth among the Hainan house churches continued at a phenomenal rate. The leaders of the movement kept detailed records of the number of churches and conversions, and the results were staggering.

In April 1998 the total number of Christians on the island reached 55,000, but just eight months later at the end of the same year the figure had mushroomed to more than 80,000 believers. The revival was reaching its maximum velocity, and a mere 18 months later, in the summer of 2000, a detailed island-wide survey by local leaders put the number of Christians in Hainan at 360,000![10]

At the height of the revival, the approximate doubling time for Christians on the island was seven months. That is, every seven months the number of believers doubled in size.

Every part of Hainan was impacted by the revival, but the highest concentrations of believers were found in the north, south, and east of the island. The areas with the weakest Christian influence were the counties in western Hainan, where the sparse population, remote mountain villages, lack of roads, poor communications, and the high percentage of minorities combined to create extra barriers to advance the gospel.

Vision and responsibility for the completion of the Great Commission was extensively taught in the new churches. All trainers and leaders were consumed with the task of reaching the lost, and on-the-job evangelism and discipleship was at the heart of everything they did.

There was little distinction between evangelism and discipleship. All believers were expected to be disciples of Christ, and each disciple was expected to share the gospel with non-Christians.

Consequently, a passion to reach the lost flowed to every new believer, resulting in a tremendous increase in the number of Christians in a short period of time.

In a bid to keep pace with the Spirit of God, tens of thousands of Gospel tracts and booklets in Chinese were printed, audio and video cassettes were mass produced, and Christian radio broadcasts added fuel to the spiritual fire that was blazing throughout Hainan.

Last but not least, a tremendous amount of intercessory prayer was focused on Hainan. Thousands of Christians around the world were mobilized with specific prayer requests on behalf of the people of Hainan, and God moved powerfully as His people cried out in heartfelt intercessory prayer.

A new day for the Cun people

As revival spread and touched all people groups in Hainan, even unofficial groups that are not recognized by the Chinese government experienced the power of the Living God in their midst.

For countless generations, the 95,000 Cun people in the western part of the island had lived in spiritual darkness. No record exists of missionary outreach among this group, who may

A girl from the little-known Cun people group
COMIBAM

be a mix of Han and Li people, for their language shows similarities with some of the Li varieties.

In the early 1990s, a Hong Kong-based organization conducted Bible training in Guangzhou for unreached minority peoples. The students chosen to receive the training were not Christians when they came, but usually within a few weeks of being lovingly introduced to God's Word, the participants were eager to surrender their lives to Christ.

Two Cun teenagers and two adults aged about 50-years-old were invited to attend one of the Bible training courses. Although hesitant and suspicious at first, the Cun attendees were soon impressed by the genuine love of the Chinese teachers, and they opened their hearts to the gospel. After three months they returned home to Hainan, from where they penned the following letter of appreciation to the Bible teachers:

> Greetings in the matchless and precious Name of the Lord Jesus Christ!
>
> A few months ago we lived in complete darkness, staggering about like blind men. Like animals, our lives consisted only of sleep, work, and eating. We had no purpose or joy. When we arrived at the Bible course, we knew nothing of the glorious message God has revealed for mankind.
>
> When the Holy Spirit graciously lifted the veils off our eyes so that we could see Jesus, it was as if our hearts were changed forever. We felt clean inside for the first time, and were overwhelmed and astonished that God would care so much for us in our low state that He would even send His only Son to die for our sins. We cannot fathom this at all, yet it is true!
>
> God's Word has become real to us. We are like starving men who have been invited to a rich banquet. We don't know where to begin as we sample God's tasty delights! Day and night we devour His holy Word.
>
> Thank you, oh, thank you for finding us and giving us the opportunity to have eternal life and to know Jesus Christ! There

was only one part of the course that was difficult for us. We found it very hard to wait three months for the school to end, because every fiber of our beings wanted to return to Hainan and share this newfound treasure with our friends and families.

Since we reached home, many more Cun people have experienced the grace of God and we now have a small fellowship that meets in our home to pray and study God's Word. We have plans to take the message of eternal life to many more villages, and even to different people groups apart from the Cun.

Please pray for us, as we pray for you![11]

Today there are believed to be at least several thousand Cun Christians on Hainan Island, as the seed that was sown in good soil went on to produce much fruit for the kingdom of God.

Letters from Hainan

We conclude this chapter by reprinting a selection of letters that were received from Hainan by various Christian ministries during the 1990s. These precious communications reveal both the strengths and weaknesses of Christianity on the island, providing insights into believers' daily lives and personal struggles. Their letters also offer a fascinating snapshot of the ever-changing conditions experienced by the body of Christ at the time.

1992

> *I am a young Christian and I'm writing to ask you to help me grow in His grace so that I may become His faithful servant.*
>
> *Our church is increasing in number, but we are lacking in laborers. The church members are scattered over 30 miles (50 km) and some of them are from the Kim Mun minority who live in the mountains. We gather at three meeting points, but there is no*

full-time leader among us. It is the young people who are responsible for preaching and training. I am one of them. I need you to help me become a good teacher.[12]

1996

I have been a Christian for six years and am responsible for a church of 90 people. I am also married with two children. There are many difficulties in leading the church, but the elders and I faithfully evangelize. Due to a kidney problem, I have little time to study the Bible. I really need some reference tools to help me make the most of my time and to counter the influence of various cults that are prevalent in our area.[13]

Please pray for me. I am ashamed to admit that since I was saved in 1993, I have not done anything for the family of God. May God revive me and give me strength and wisdom to do His work.[14]

1997

I often accompany my church elders when they visit the villages in our county, telling people about Christ and His kingdom, helping them to accept the Savior. However, many of them are idol wor-shippers who refuse to forsake their idols. Others are atheists who only believe in evolution.[15]

1999

I was an atheist and I used to be very antagonistic toward Christianity, but since listening to your program I have changed my attitude and have even contemplated believing in Christ. However, there is only one elderly Christian lady and no young believers in my village. I admit that I am a person of weak faith. Whenever people question the benefit or reason in choosing a foreign god over the myriad of Chinese gods, I waver in making a commitment to Christ.[16]

Before I turned to Jesus, I was a rogue who indulged in gambling and whoring. In 1988 I got a job in Hainan, and although I earned much money, it all vanished because of gambling. In 1996 the gospel was preached to my work team, but I rejected it.

Two years later I returned to my home village to do farm work. While there, I attended a revival meeting and felt God tell me that now was the time I must be saved. On the fifth day, God made His redemption and salvation clear to me. I was convicted and repented of my sins. When I placed my burdens and sins on Jesus Christ, tears rolled down my cheeks. I hated my bad character and was grateful to the Lord for His forgiveness. I heard the Holy Spirit tell me that I was forgiven and to stop sinning.

From that time until now I have lived a new life and have stopped gambling, drinking, and fighting. When I told my workmates that I believe in Jesus Christ they thought I was kidding, but when they witnessed the change in my words and behavior they were amazed and admitted that God really can change a person. My old self has died, and I am now living for Jesus Christ.[17]

When Heaven Came to Hainan

A key conversion

Although he described himself as an introvert, the Baptist missionary often went on prayer walks in his city. This gave him an opportunity to practice speaking Chinese while meeting new people. Soon, locals began to recognize him as he did his rounds, and as they gradually opened up and shared some of the struggles in their lives and families, he asked if he could pray for them. Almost invariably, people were thankful to be prayed for, and many sensed the presence of Jesus Christ when their needs were presented before Him.

It was during one prayer walk that the seeds of a key spiritual transformation took place, as the missionary recalled:

> I saw a lady who had been my language teacher for a while. She was a highly educated woman, which was rare in Hainan at the time. Most people only attended school to the fourth grade before dropping out. She was also a member of the Communist Party, so was well known and respected in the community.
>
> As we talked, she mentioned a work problem she was having, and I offered to pray for her. Being a Communist Party member meant she was an avowed atheist, but she didn't want to hurt my feelings so she agreed to let me pray.
>
> I prayed for her workplace problem, and then for her, her husband and their young daughter, and I asked the Lord Jesus to bless their health and finances according to His will. At the end of my prayer she did something very culturally unusual. She grabbed my arm and said, "Thank you so much! That was very meaningful. Something strange and wonderful happened that I

have never experienced before. The whole time you were praying, I felt an intense peace and love like I've never felt before."

We parted ways, but the next day I was out prayer walking again and saw the same lady. She gave me an update on her work situation, and then asked, "Can you please pray for me again?"

I again prayed for her and her family, but this time I expanded my prayers to include the local community, the city, Hainan

More than 300,000 people in Hainan surrendered their lives to Jesus Christ in the 1990s
IMB

Island, the whole of China, and even for some international events that were happening at the time.

I probably prayed for 20 minutes, until I couldn't think of anything else to pray for. When I finally finished she said, "It happened again. The whole time you were praying I felt an intense love and peace." Then she asked me, "Does God really care about all those things you just prayed for?"

This gave me an opportunity to share more of the gospel, so I replied, "Yes, God cares about all these things. He is the Creator, and He cares about everything that goes on in His creation. Jesus even said He cares about sparrows that fall from the sky, and He knows the number of hairs on your head. He possesses all wisdom and knowledge, and He has all power and authority in heaven and on earth. God is not confined to time and space, and in Jesus Christ all things in the universe hold together."

Next, she asked, "Can I also pray?"

I replied, "You can pray any time and God will hear you, but it won't be the same feeling as when I pray. You see, I have a relationship with God and I have been adopted as His child. He doesn't have that kind of relationship with you, so He has no obligation to you. The good news, however, is that you can also have this kind of special relationship with God."

I spent considerable time sharing the Scriptures with her, starting in Genesis and leading to the death and resurrection of Jesus. I did so in such a way that focused on God's plans to have relationships with people. When I finished, I asked if she wanted to pray to receive Christ and to begin a new life as an adopted child of the King of Kings. She replied, "No. If I was to do that, I would almost certainly lose my job and I would be kicked out of the Communist Party. When my husband found out, he would leave me and would take our daughter. I'm sorry, but I'm just not prepared to make those sacrifices."

As we parted that day, she asked, "Can I teach my daughter to pray?" I explained that she could teach her, but it also wouldn't be the same because she too didn't have a special relationship with God. She said she understood and thanked me.

Several weeks passed before I met her again. When she saw me from a distance, she ran toward me with her face beaming. In tropical Hainan, people never run for any reason, as it's always hot and humid. I knew it had to be important, and the first words out of her mouth were, "I, too, am now a child of God!"

In the weeks since our last conversation, she had taught her six-year-old daughter how to pray, and they had prayed about many things together each day.

One afternoon the mother and daughter were in line to purchase raffle tickets to help disabled children. In China there was little or no compassion for the disabled. Most people just wished they would go away and die. As she stood in line, however, the important Communist Party member found herself praying out loud, "Dear Lord, thank you that you love these disabled people. No one else loves them, but you care about every detail of their lives, because you created them. Please bless these children and give them good health. I thank you that you have granted my family sound bodies and minds, and I pray you will do the same for these children. Amen."

She went home, and as she lay on her bed that night, it suddenly dawned on her that everything she had prayed was true. God really had blessed her and her family, and He truly was the only one who cared about the disabled and downtrodden members of society.

Next, she told me, "I remembered what you said about how someone can enter into a special relationship with God through Jesus Christ. I realized that I needed to know this wonderful God. I wanted to serve Him and to be His child. I chose to follow Jesus, and I led my daughter to do the same thing."[1]

This mother and daughter became two of the earliest believers among the Hainanese people group. From that small beginning, the movement grew to become a massive revival that brought hundreds of thousands of people into a special relationship with the Living God.

A blank canvas in the hands of God

Throughout history, God has visited people in various parts of the world with great power, transforming multitudes of people in a short space of time. Sometimes revivals are referred to as awakenings or renewals—when the Lord Jesus Christ visits His people and refreshes them in preparation for a new work of grace.

While renewals can be said to directly benefit the church, all true visitations of God flow out of the churches and into the surrounding communities, where sinners are convicted of their transgressions and come to faith in Christ. J. Edwin Orr, a revivalist and author, made this distinction between normal evangelism and God-sent revival:

> The Lord Jesus observed that the wind blows where it wills; and so it is with the Spirit. No individual or organization of people can arrange or produce an outpouring of the Spirit. It is exclusively the work of God. Believers understand it most imperfectly; anthropologists, psychologists and sociologists cannot explain it away; cannot explain it at all....
>
> One cannot see the invisible wind, but one can see what the force of the wind can accomplish. No one can measure the outpouring of the Holy Spirit, but it is often possible to see what the outpouring of the Spirit has accomplished. History records what the outpouring of the Spirit has achieved in the reviving of the Church and the awakening of the people, resulting in evangelizing of inquirers and teaching of disciples, and, by many or by few, the reforming of society.[2]

Some revivals in history are well-documented, such as the Welsh Revival of the early twentieth century, when approximately 100,000 people were added to the churches of Wales. It then spread into England and Scotland, with about one million people surrendering their lives to the Son of God.[3]

At the height of the Second Great Awakening in the United States prior to the Civil War, revivalist Charles Finney is said to have led up to 50,000 people to repentance and faith in a single week;[4] while back at the dawn of Christianity, the first believers were so mightily used by God that the people of Thessalonica cried out, "These men who have caused trouble all over the world have now come here" (Acts 17:6b).

Without question, the numerically greatest revival in Christian history has occurred in China in the past 50 years, and it serves as the driving force behind The China Chronicles series you are reading. More than 100 million people in China have come to Christ since the advent of Communism in 1949, despite (or rather, aided by) decades of intense persecution.

The tendency of fallen mankind is to attribute all progress to human endeavor, but true revivals have little to do with the work of men, and much to do with a supernatural outpouring of the Holy Spirit. For a time, heaven comes down to earth, and resistance to the will of God is blown away like a cardboard shack in the face of a hurricane.

Visitations from heaven invariably leave unconverted people completely baffled and unable to grasp what has happened in their midst. So it was in Hainan, where the atheist leaders appeared flummoxed by the revival. They could not perceive the source of the transformation, nor could they see any wind. But they observed the massive impact the Holy Spirit had upon Hainan's society.

One of the main characteristics of the revival in Hainan during the 1990s and beyond was simplicity. The Christians involved with the movement were determined to implement biblical Christianity. For that to happen, they carefully studied the Bible and found that countless beliefs and practices of churches around the world are not based on the New Testament pattern of church life, but are man-made traditions and denominational rules. These may have an appearance of godliness, but in reality they prohibit the flow of the Holy Spirit and result in dead formalism and legalism, instead of rivers of living water flowing out from the body of Christ to the communities they serve.

Before the Hainan revival began, a determined decision was made to strip away all non-essential religious forms. There was no distinction between clergy and "lay" Christians, and each child of God was a soul-winner and disciple-maker. All believers had an important role to play, and their diverse spiritual gifts benefitted the whole body of Christ.

Some people may assume that the revival that swept Hainan was the result of the implementation of a highly complex methodology, but the training given to people was extremely simple and Bible-based.

Crucially, it should be understood that those who were engaged in "full-time ministry" for Christ were not moved to the side or pushed down. Rather, all believers were raised up so that all Christians, from the youngest to the oldest, were full-time ministers of the gospel. The former tendency for such roles to be performed by a special "class" of Christian was discarded.

In a sense, because the church in Hainan was so small before the revival started, from the commencement of their Christian journeys most new believers did not have "baggage" from prior church traditions and experiences that they needed to discard. As far as they were concerned, the pattern of Christian life they experienced was normal, and they assumed that Christians all around the world lived and worshipped God the same way.

The results in Hainan were astonishing, as God had a blank canvas upon which to paint a masterpiece. He did so, transforming hundreds of thousands of lives in every segment of Hainan society.

Shared leadership

The training process that helped spur the revival in Hainan began with just three house churches, totaling less than 100 members. As the leaders were trained to evangelize the lost, they were encouraged to focus on the neediest areas of the island where there were no existing churches.

The small number of churches in Hainan that had been established prior to the revival were encouraged to send evangelists to places and people groups that had never received a gospel witness. Many of those churches were filled with second, third, or fourth generation believers who had lost their passion for Christ and had little or no vision to reach the lost. Most pastors had become preoccupied with the immediate needs of their flocks and had no desire to look beyond their own backyards.

When the sleeping churches were encouraged to go into unreached parts of the island, however, they received a bolt of energy from the Holy Spirit and were motivated to do whatever was necessary to see Christ glorified among all the people of Hainan.

Revival took most Hainan believers out of structured churches and into informal settings where everyone had a role to play in the body of Christ
RCMI

Also, short-term mission teams from nations like Malaysia, Singapore, Hong Kong, and Taiwan provided direction and foundational teaching to the fledgling churches in Hainan. They laid a solid theological foundation for the new believers, so that most people who were converted to Christ in the revival remained faithful to the Lord. A report noted the efforts of the overseas Chinese Christians:

> Leadership training teams from Hong Kong, Taiwan and Singapore went to assist in the process, and fruit resulted. After these efforts had been underway for almost two years the churches began sending church planting teams. Their efforts were not random. They set about to systematically cover the island with a network of cooperating churches. They sent teams to the areas with the least witness to make sure the gospel was available in all parts of the province and to every language group. Within eight months they had planted 14 new churches in the most difficult and resistant areas.[5]

An important principle that created a springboard for the Hainan revival was "shared leadership" (i.e., leaders were not allowed to become dictators to their flocks but were required to practice mutual accountability with other leaders). In this way, each fellowship remained healthy because of the input of new ideas, fresh teaching, and the balanced acceptance of different spiritual gifts.

Teaching was imparted in such a way that poorly educated and illiterate people did not feel left behind. Pastors were required to be unpaid volunteers, and meetings were held in believers' homes rather than church buildings. Consequently, despite believers' meager salaries, money was available to send evangelists and church planters throughout the island, while the financial needs of church members were also met.

The love Christians had for one another, and for non-believers, was a powerful testimony to the people of Hainan. God's children even shared their financial resources with strangers in need—something rarely seen in modern, materialistic China. This stark contrast and display of selflessness attracted thousands of people to Jesus Christ.

Whenever new churches were planted, multiple leaders were immediately identified and appointed by the other members of the flock. This enabled the churches to grow without excessive outside influence, and prevented a leadership vacuum from occurring should one or two leaders be arrested.

Another factor that fanned the revival fires in Hainan was the implicit trust placed in new believers by church leaders. Because of the excesses of the Cultural Revolution, little or no trust was placed in people by the leaders of Chinese society. Common people were forced to obey Communist Party policy or suffer severe consequences and to blindly submit to their political leaders. China had become a deeply untrusting society, where hundreds of millions of people felt they could only believe in themselves. The trust given to new Christians in the Hainan revival was therefore particularly liberating to many people who had been oppressed their whole lives.

When a household displayed an interest or had already accepted Christ, their family members and friends were invited to attend Bible studies. In this way, the base of interested people grew ever wider. After a few weeks of simple witness, an invitation was given for people to believe. Those who decided for Christ immediately joined a basic discipleship program which lasted a few weeks. Upon completion of the program the new believers were baptized.

Church planters identified which of the new converts were potential leaders after taking careful note of each person's integrity, character, and hunger for God's Word. Soon, all public meetings were turned over to them.

The evangelists, meanwhile, stayed behind to mentor the new leaders, advising them how to deal with problems in the church and teaching them God's Word, which they immediately taught to new believers. In this way, the movement was completely localized and grew naturally. Because the church leaders were already known and respected in their communities, Jesus Christ was revered and accepted as a positive influence. Critics could never charge that Christianity was a Western religion because the movement was completely led and funded by local Hainanese people.

After a house church had become firmly established, it was required to divide into smaller groups, according to the security concerns in each area. In cities and towns, house groups never exceeded 30 members, although in rural areas where the police presence was less threatening, congregations often grew to hundreds of believers.

Most churches met twice a week, including once on Sunday when non-believers were welcome to attend. An additional mid-week service, held exclusively for believers, concentrated on discipleship, training, and receiving strategies from God.

After a while, house church leaders in each county gathered on the first day of every lunar month for a day of prayer, fasting, and training, while on the 15th day of every lunar month church leaders throughout the entire province gathered in one place for unified prayer and fasting.

Attending these gatherings came at great personal cost to most of the church leaders. They were so poor that to afford the bus fares, many of them fasted for a week prior to the meetings, and used the money they would otherwise have spent on food to buy bus tickets. In the subsistence economy of Hainan at the time, they literally gave all they had for the gospel, and these strategic meetings were pivotal in the whole island being saturated with the gospel. When the church leaders connected with each other, they became aware of the big picture of what God was doing, and they returned home deeply encouraged with stories to tell their fellow believers.

Stories from the Frontlines

In any place that receives a mighty visitation of God, countless testimonies emerge of how the power of the Holy Spirit healed, delivered, and saved those who were captives of sin and Satan. Across Hainan hundreds of thousands of people were radically transformed in the revival. In this chapter we recount just a handful of significant incidents that occurred, which reveal the redemptive grace and power of Jesus Christ.

The Qigong master's defeat

As powerful revival spread throughout Hainan, the forces of darkness predictably rose in opposition and tried to snuff out the movement. Christ's followers, however, learned to stand in the full armor of God and battle against these insidious dark forces, emerging victorious on many occasions.

After being developed millennia ago as part of traditional Chinese medicine, Qigong (pronounced "chee-gong") had gained great popularity among millions of people in China. Although in Western nations today it is merely considered a helpful breathing and exercise regime, in China it has morphed to include a dark spiritual element characterized by powerful encounters, miracles, healings, and unusual events.

In the modern era, Qigong proved increasingly attractive to multitudes of people in China who were hungry for a spiritual reality to fill the void created by Communism. Mass meetings by Qigong masters were often held in sports stadiums and other large arenas, attended by huge crowds of 50,000 people or more.

Although Qigong has many forms, the type "which is extremely popular in Hainan involves very clear demon possession. In daily meditation the goal is to 'lose control' of your body and become animated by a spirit which is one's 'keeper.'"[1]

Because Qigong is not an organized religion, its practitioners were not considered a direct threat to Communist ideology. It consequently became popular even at the top levels of Chinese government, and political leaders were seen on television attending Qigong exhibitions. One source noted, "A form of Qigong involving definite demon possession also has a pervasive influence, dominating government officials and university faculty but reaching down to the rural areas as well."[2]

A Qigong master named Zhang Zhixiang decided the benefits of Qigong should be made available to all Chinese, so he founded a school in his home province of Hubei and gathered a group of disciples. Soon, thousands of people expressed a desire to be trained in the secret arts, and Zhang's school grew rapidly as he

Practitioners at a Qigong school in China
Nick Ledger

reinvested all the profits earned from tuition fees back into his training institute.

Zhang desired to have a trained Qigong practitioner in every household throughout China, so that their spiritual "energy" would care for the other family members. Children were taught to chant and meditate so they might enjoy the "benefits" for themselves.

A small group of Hainanese attended Zhang's school in 1990 and returned to the island eager to spread his teaching. Through those disciples, Hainan became the place where most of Zhang's followers lived. Among them were many people in high positions, including Haikou City officials and Public Security chiefs. Leading government workers and almost all university faculty members had been trained in Qigong principles.

In 1992, Zhang decided to visit Hainan to hold exhibitions, where he would heal the sick and perform signs and wonders. In the days before he arrived, a massive crime-wave erupted across the island. Nobody understood what was happening. Mass murders, gang rapes, and every conceivable act of demonic filth took place.

Thousands of families were affected in peculiar ways. Many became so desperate for assistance that they visited anyone they thought might have spiritual power to help them. They flocked to Buddhist monks, Daoist priests, and Christian pastors, saying they had family members who had suddenly become demon-possessed. They begged the religious leaders to free their loved ones from the evil powers that had seized them.

In Hainan, the wave of interest in Qigong coincided with the start of the Christian revival, and when news of the Qigong master's visit emerged, a ministry launched an intercessory prayer initiative, with believers mobilized throughout Hainan and around the world to fast and pray against the evil powers behind Qigong. A newsletter was sent out with the following requests:

Pray for the breaking down of spiritual strongholds, the dethroning of principalities and powers, for the protection of children, and for God's light to expose the falsehoods and half-truths of the adversary. Pray for a "power encounter" on a large scale to show God's superior strength and for the protection of Christian families.

Pray for the discrediting of the Qigong movement's leaders and trainers through illness (to which they are supposedly impervious) or some other means. Pray for their conversion.

Pray for the binding of spiritual forces of darkness from those who are spiritually hungry and for the full spiritual armor outfitting, discernment, wisdom, and safety for Christians on the front lines of this battle.[3]

Many Christians responded by crying out to the Lord Jesus Christ, and He answered the fervent prayers of His people.

Much of Hainan Island seemed to buzz with anticipation in the days leading up to the Qigong master's visit. The government closed a large market area in downtown Haikou and turned it into a meeting place. A stage and floodlights were erected, and a massive crowd turned up. Zhang Zhixiang was touted as being able to levitate in public view, and he reputedly had the power to heal all kinds of diseases. It was even announced that he would make his body supernaturally glow during the night meeting.

That night, after he mounted the stage before thousands of adoring spectators and followers, Zhang was completely powerless, and he couldn't do any miracles at all. No one was healed, and he was unable to levitate. The meeting was a huge flop. According to a report of Zhang's trip to Hainan,

Zhang tried to heal a deaf-mute boy in dramatic fashion and failed, which was quite an embarrassment. Similarly, the top Qigong practitioner in the province had the lights turned off in a meeting so she could demonstrate her supernatural ability to make her body glow. She too failed and the people mocked her.

When Zhang traveled down the east coast of the island, he stopped at Wenchang to hold a meeting in the town hall. The local officials, however, suddenly changed their minds and he was no longer welcome. Instead, a county official obtained the use of the local school building. Zhang said, "I sense a spiritual opposition here...but we will have the meeting anyway." When the official who acquired the use of the building was climbing a ladder to put up special lights, he suddenly fell to the floor dead. The meeting was cancelled.[4]

Zhang Zhixiang returned to mainland China after his unsuccessful Hainan experience. Although his meetings had failed because of Christians' fervent intercession, a real estate developer on the island gave him one million Yuan ($170,000) to expand his institute in Hainan, and a new Qigong school was constructed at Tunchang.

A teenage girl's triumph and tragedy

In a related story, the highest-ranked Qigong master in Hainan at the time was a woman who was also the piano instructor at Haikou University.

Every year a prestigious piano competition was held in Hong Kong, which was broadcast throughout China on national television. That year a 19-year-old Christian girl from Hainan won the competition.

As soon as the winner was announced, the television interviewers crowded around the piano instructor, asking how she had been able to train such a great talent. The woman replied that her success was due to her being a Qigong master. She proudly boasted, "I give all my students amulets to wear, and I teach them how to meditate. I also give them Qigong blessings to help them outperform their competitors."

The teenage girl who won the competition was a member of a church in Haikou. She felt intimidated by her teacher, but when she heard the Name of Jesus Christ being dishonored on national television, she couldn't remain silent. She stepped in

A house church prayer meeting in Hainan
RCMI

front of her teacher and boldly proclaimed, "This is not true! I am a Christian! I have never used this woman's amulets and I have never practiced Qigong. I was able to win this competition because the Lord God, my Creator, has given me the abilities and honored my hard work to serve Him and glorify His Name."[5]

After the Christian girl returned to Hainan, she was blacklisted from attending university. She paid a dear price for her bold stand for the Lord, but this was just the beginning of trouble in her life.

One evening she was badly injured in a terrible car crash, which left her in a deep coma. In China, sickness or injury are often attributed to a person's bad karma, and consequently little compassion is shown to them. All the comatose girl's friends deserted her, and her boyfriend stole all her money and possessions. The Haikou Hospital even refused to treat her in the emergency room because she had no money.

It later emerged that the crash had not been an accident at all, but a targeted hit-and-run, probably orchestrated by the Qigong woman who felt she had been publicly humiliated by her Christian student on television.

In God's providence, Christians heard about the desperate girl and arranged to pay her medical bills from their own meager resources. The doctors examined her and offered no hope, declaring that if she lived, the massive brain damage she had suffered would leave her in a vegetative state for the rest of her life.

Two Christian nurses, whose lives had been transformed in the revival, decided to visit and pray for her every day. They read the Bible over her and took care of her medical needs, cleaning her and providing physical therapy several times a day.

The nurses also contacted the girl's family, and two of her sisters traveled from another province to help care for her. They were amazed by the prayers, Bible reading, and loving care they witnessed from the Christians, and they surrendered their lives to Jesus.

After a while the money ran out, and the hospital sent the girl home to die. The two sisters took her to the place they had rented and waited for the end. Finally, when they were at the point of giving up and had decided to let her starve to death, they tried one more thing.

Because she had been such an accomplished musician before the accident, they carried her limp body and sat her down on a piano bench, placing her fingers on the keys. Suddenly, without warning, she came out of the coma! Everyone who saw it was amazed and humbled, and they realized a great miracle had taken place.

Two days later the girl took her first steps, and within a week it was clear that she was on the road to recovery. The girl and her entire family knew it was the prayers of the Christians that had resulted in this great act of mercy from God.

Despite this great miracle, her life continued to be a daily struggle. Due to the neurological injuries she had received, she was never able to play the piano at the same level again, and the Hainan authorities—still angry that she had mentioned Jesus Christ on national television—further punished her by refusing to let her get a job of any description. Thankfully, the local Christians continued to care for her, and she was a living witness to the power and love of Jesus Christ.

When God would not let His name be defamed

A powerful testimony merged in November 1995 after house church Christians traveled to a village in Lingao County in northern Hainan. When the believers began to preach the gospel, the locals declared there was no way they would ever believe in the Christian God because they already worshipped the most powerful spirits.

The people issued a stern warning to the evangelists, saying that six years earlier the village shaman had received a vision that Christianity was the one true religion. The man was so convinced that he immediately burned all his spirit charms and other paraphernalia, even though he had not yet heard the gospel and was not a believer.

The moment he did this, the people said the shaman saw a vision where many demons flew at him and attempted to destroy him. He was so terrified that he tore his clothes off, ran around naked, and went insane. He also lost his ability to speak. The man picked up stones and threw them into the air, trying to hit the demons that were tormenting him. He lived in a hut with a thatch roof and walls, so his rock throwing and other antics soon demolished his roof, and he was forced to live in the middle of the four walls which were the only part of the structure still standing.

The shaman's life became pitiful. He was exposed to the elements, naked, unable to speak, and completely tormented by demons. He survived only by the kindness of his neighbors, who brought him food to eat.

The villagers said that the shaman's experiences were proof that their local spirits were more powerful than the Christian God, so they told the evangelists not to waste their time, for they would only become Christians if Jesus was able to heal and deliver the tormented man.

The house church evangelists were new believers and they didn't know what to do, so they returned home, much to the derision of the villagers.

After hearing about the unsuccessful trip, the church began to pray and fast for this village and for the shaman, asking God to glorify His Name because Jesus Christ was being defamed.

After the evangelists were shown what the Bible says about delivering demonized people, they returned to the village and cast the demons out of the tormented man. He immediately regained his speech, and they clothed him and helped rebuild his home.

After hearing the gospel, the shaman dedicated his life to Jesus Christ, and when they saw the tremendous change in his life, almost the entire village became Christian. The new believers then took the gospel to the neighboring village, and most people there also repented of their sins and placed their trust in the Living God.

As a testimony to God's power over the forces of darkness, the new Christians began to meet for worship and Bible study in the home of the ex-shaman. His powerful, life-changing experience was the catalyst for many people to come into the kingdom of God, and the Name of Jesus was rightfully honored among the people in that area.

"We just prayed!"

One of the more remarkable stories of how God used humble, simple-hearted Christians to establish His kingdom in Hainan was related by author Carl Lawrence.[6]

In the mid-1990s, two young women in another province believed in Christ after they heard the gospel via a shortwave radio broadcast. The duo received Bibles and immediately wanted to serve God with all their hearts. A Hong Kong-based pastor encouraged them to remain where they were and minister to their neighbors, but the girls protested, "No! The Bible you gave us says Jesus commanded us to go into all the world. We must go!"

The pastor, feeling ashamed by his own comparative lack of zeal, relented and told the girls there was a need for workers on

Hainan Island. They had never heard of Hainan, but were certain God wanted them to preach the gospel there.

Two years later the girls returned to the Chinese mainland where the Hong Kong pastor met them and introduced them to several visiting Western church leaders. He had not heard any news since their departure for Hainan. When the girls were asked about their work and whether they had been able to start any churches, Lawrence recalled,

> The women put their heads down and answered, "Oh pastor, we have only been there two years...yea, two years. Not many. Not very many." Their voices were apologetic. "We have only been there a short time. The people were not very friendly, no, not very friendly. Sometimes they became very vicious. Yes, sometimes they told us they were going to drown us in the ocean. Several men threatened us. Oh my, and because we were so young, even some of the ladies did not like us. Yes, some even called us terrible names...so not many churches...no, not many."[7]

*Fervent prayer meetings are a hallmark
of house church believers in Hainan*
RCMI

Finally, after being asked again by the pastor, the girls admitted they had been able to start 30 churches during their two years in Hainan!

The pastor and his Western friends were surprised by the news. They asked how many people attended their new churches. After again going through a process of self-effacing apologies, they replied, "Two hundred and twenty." The listeners assumed the girls meant they had a total of 220 converts in their 30 churches, but 220 was the number of members in the smallest of the churches!

"How many people do you have in the largest of your churches?" the pastor demanded to know. "Oh...not many.... Less than 5,000. Only 4,900. Yes, less than 5,000. We have just started."[8]

The Westerners were so touched by the humility and zeal of the two young ladies that they began to weep. One of the visitors told the pastor to ask the ladies how they managed to achieve such great results.

> "What did we do? Why nothing. Yes, we did nothing.... Nothing."
>
> The amazed onlookers protested, "You did nothing? You have 30 churches—the smallest with 220 people, the largest with almost 5,000! And you did nothing?"
>
> The two evangelists replied, "We just prayed.... After we prayed, the Holy Spirit would tell us exactly what to do. We would keep praying and He would tell us what to do, and we would do it. Then we would pray again, and He would tell us what to do next."[9]

Another source shared some additional background information and a fresh perspective on the two ladies' experiences during their two-year adventure with God in Hainan:

> When they arrived, they didn't know what to do so they just started praying. That was alright for a while but soon they started to get hungry. They had no money and prayer didn't fill their

stomachs. They started working, helping the local ladies with their laundry and taking care of their children. As they worked, they sang gospel songs. Soon the local people began to ask them about the songs they were singing. They shared their faith and people believed. Soon everyone in the village had heard so the two ladies moved on.

After less than two years the ladies returned home. In 20 months, they had started 21 new groups with nearly 9,000 people involved. They had to meet out in open fields because the groups were so large.[10]

The two young women had been tremendously successful evangelists in the face of great opposition and had successfully planted many churches in several counties near Sanya City in southern Hainan. However, because of an almost total lack of discipleship, much of the fruit was lost to cults in subsequent years, so that by 1999 perhaps only 5,000 of the duo's converts remained true believers.

Grounded in the Word of God

As the church in Hainan experienced rapid growth in the 1990s and beyond, an inevitable concern arose from some overseas Christians, who feared that rapid growth during revival was likely to result in an infestation of heresy.

Although the above story of the two young evangelists may accentuate those concerns, overall in Hainan the revival during the 1990s was tremendously successful in establishing long-term believers who were grounded in the Word of God. The difference was that whereas the two women were new believers with a great zeal only for evangelism, most of the revival movement that swept Hainan was based on in-depth discipleship training and multiplication.

The Hainan revival—along with 12 other contemporary mass people movements to Christ around the world—were studied by a selection of researchers from different Evangelical backgrounds, who found that no significant heresies had infested the movements.[11]

Ironically, the researchers concluded that the traditional style of church leadership in much of the world—where one or a small number of pastors do all the Bible teaching in a church, is a structure far more likely to result in the introduction and spread of false teaching.

In Hainan, although there were certainly many early problems related to the rapid advance of the gospel, the model of shared leadership among suitable believers with good character proved to be a far safer—and more biblical—model for healthy church growth. With many church members saved and renewed by God's Word, any hint of false teaching in Hainan was much more quickly confronted and corrected by groups of believers than is possible when power is held by a few individuals.

To this day, the Hainan revival remains Bible-centered and Christ-exalting, whereas (as you will read in the next chapter on the Li people), on those occasions during the missionary era when one or two individuals felt they alone were called to be the interpreters of God's truth, woeful corruptions of Christian doctrine and practice occurred.

Intense spiritual warfare

During the Hainan revival of the last 30 years, miracles and signs and wonders have occurred at regular intervals, helping add fuel to the flames and convincing thousands of the truth of the gospel and the all-encompassing power of Jesus Christ.

During times of great revival it is normal for people to focus on dramatic conversions, healings, and growth of the church.

What often gets overlooked, however, are the struggles and suf-ferings the chosen vessels of God are called to endure.

> One American missionary, whom God used to introduce a pow-erful discipleship movement throughout Hainan, maintained a low profile while he lived on the island. Years later, however, the missionary shared some of the personal struggles and attacks he and his family experienced, as Satan sought to blunt the Lord's chosen instruments and prevent the revival from expanding.

On one occasion, the missionary and a new Chinese believer boarded a bus to another county. After prayerfully committing their journey to the Lord, they were disappointed to miss the daily express bus by five minutes, and they were forced to endure a ride on a slow local bus, which would take eight hours across terrible, potholed roads.

After agreeing that the slower bus would give them more time to talk about the things of God, they commenced their trip. About an hour later they passed the express bus, which had been in a collision and was lying upside down on the side of the road. They were suddenly thankful that they had missed the express bus that day. Then, a short distance further, a man dressed in camouflage uniform and holding an automatic weapon forced the bus to stop.

> He was a member of an independent militia. He walked down the aisle of the bus to where we were sitting, looked around, and then got off the bus without saying a word.
>
> This stimulated much discussion not only between my com-panion and I, but also among the other passengers. No one could understand why the militiaman did not rob the passengers, especially the foreigner and the well-dressed local man who was traveling with him.
>
> We continued on our way, but about an hour later a gang of four men stopped the bus and boarded it. One had a gun and the other possessed a large knife. They came to where we were sitting

and intentionally surrounded us, with one man on our left, one on our right, one in front, and one behind. I tried to engage the leader in conversation, but he wasn't interested so I left him alone. About 10 miles (16 km) down the road all four men got off the bus without incident.

This time the other passengers were buzzing. Everyone said the men were members of a well-known murderous gang, and it was unbelievable that we had escaped with both our lives and our money. I realized these incidents provided an ideal opportunity. Not only did it build up my young traveling companion's faith, but it was also a powerful witness to every person riding on the bus.[12]

On another occasion, the same Baptist missionary was out jogging one morning in a rural area of Hainan when he recalled,

I turned a corner when I noticed a jeep driving toward me down the dirt road. The driver was honking and flashing his lights. I thought he wanted me to get off the road, so I started running on the shoulder. Suddenly, I felt compelled to turn around. As I did so, a vicious German Shepherd launched itself at my throat. It was a trained military attack dog that had suddenly gone berserk and escaped from his trainer. He attacked me silently just as he had been trained.

I had no time to react or defend myself, but an amazing thing happened. As the dog launched at my throat, it crumpled in mid-air just as if it had hit a glass wall. The dog fell to the ground dazed and confused, and his trainer appeared down the road, calling him off me. I have no doubt that an angel protected me that day.[13]

The missionary's family, meanwhile, also experienced strong demonic attacks. His wife began to experience severe back problems which the doctors said were normally only caused by trauma. The pain intensified and caused virtual paralysis, which required major surgery.

Strangely, the pioneer couple's two-year-old son suddenly began to fall down when he walked. He had learned to walk when he was seven months old, but now was having trouble. His father followed him around and observed that when he fell,

> it was always just as if someone was holding his foot to the ground when he was trying to take a step. When I asked him what had happened that is exactly what he told me, "Daddy, someone was holding my foot down." It happened several times near broken glass or stairs. Fortunately, he was never seriously hurt.[14]

Through these and many other incidents that displayed God's protective power, the Hainan revival continued to spread, until there was scarcely a village anywhere on the island where the praises of Jesus Christ were not heard ringing out from deeply appreciative, redeemed Christians who just a short time earlier had never heard the gospel.

In 1996, the American Baptist missionary and his family who had lived in Hainan for five years sensed that their key role in the revival movement had drawn to a close, and they left the island. He said,

> I felt that we were no longer necessary. The local believers were doing very well, but if we stayed I felt there would be a danger of developing unhealthy dependency on us. I made sure church leaders had people they could go to if they had questions, and we moved on to our next adventure with the Lord, although Hainan will always hold a very precious place in our hearts.[15]

The Li

A Li woman weaving by traditional methods
Valery Bocman

The ancestors of the more than 1.2 million Li people in Hainan are recognized as the original inhabitants of the island, having migrated from south China more than 2,000 years ago. Although no significant communities of Li are found on the Chinese mainland today, their language is part of the Tai linguistic family, indicating a historical relationship between the Li and other minority groups in south China such as the Bouyei, Dong, Shui, and Zhuang.

The Li people have a rich oral history, which is handed down from one generation to the next. In 1937, a visitor interviewed Li elders and was told the following story of a worldwide flood and the origins of the Li people:

> In ancient times there was a flood which submerged all the world. All mankind drowned except a sister and brother who escaped the disaster. Since they were brother and sister, it was impossible for them to marry, and they dispersed to east and west to seek mates. They met again without finding anybody. The same attempt was repeated and again failed. Aware of this trouble, the Thunder god transformed himself into a human being, came down, and told the brother, "I came here as a witness. You two may become man and wife."[1]

Today, the Li in Hainan divide into five distinct subgroups, each with their own dress, customs, and dialect. The largest of the sub-tribes is the Ha (687,000 people), followed by the Qi (314,000), Jiamao (92,000), Bendi (79,000), and Meifu (53,000). Because of their cultural and linguistic differences, each should be considered distinct people groups that God desires to reach with the gospel of Jesus Christ.

For centuries, interactions between the Li and the Han Chinese were fractious. The Li saw themselves as the masters of their own land and strongly resisted attempts to subdue them, while the Han viewed the Li as "backward" and rebellious. As a result of this ethnic tension, in 1933 "a dozen Li people were captured and exhibited at the zoo in iron cages. They were said to be 'born of monkeys and raised by snakes.'"[2]

Early missionaries who ventured into the dangerous interior regions of Hainan tended to separate the Li into "Wild" and "Tame" subgroups. Presbyterian William Leverett wrote in 1900,

> The Wild Li, who inhabit the mountainous interior of the island, live a wild life, and are still in tribal relations. Tribe differs from tribe in dialect, in the pattern tattooed on the women, and, when they come up to market, in the style of coat and skirt they wear. The men, except for different modes of doing up their hair, behold each other on their native heath, differing only as God made

them to differ. Without doubt, the Wild Li, even within 30 miles of Nada, belong to several different tribes.[3]

Foreign visitors who dared to enter the Li mountains were rare, and the fierce reputation of the tribesmen meant that hiring a local guide who was willing to take them into the interior was almost impossible. When American explorer Leonard Clark ventured into Li territory in 1938, he reported,

> I was totally unarmed. Before the expedition started I had been warned that this was safer, since the Li might slip into our camp in the night and cut our throats for our rifles and pistols.
>
> Throughout this Ha Li country the headmen insisted that I be supplied with bodyguards while camping near their villages. They feared that a neighboring village might send assassins to murder us so that the village would be held responsible and be made the object of attack from a Chinese punitive expedition.
>
> I saw the charred remains of one luckless village, punished for robbery. Hundreds of empty machine-gun shells still lay about in piles.[4]

When the Japanese army invaded Hainan in 1939, the Li joined with the Communists to repel them. Despite being hopelessly outmatched by the modern Japanese weapons and airplanes, the Li were on home turf, and used their local knowledge to launch successful guerrilla campaigns against the invaders.

The Japanese finally grew fed up with the resistance and conducted many massacres of Li people, with countless women and young girls mercilessly raped and murdered. Tens of thousands of Li people were slaughtered, which markedly reduced their population at the time.

Jungle courtship

Although Li culture has changed as Hainan opened to the outside world, for centuries the way young Li men and women found each other has remained constant. It was strictly forbidden for a Li boy to marry a girl from his own village, but if an attractive girl from a neighboring village caught his eye, he would find out where her family's hut was located and would obscure himself in the jungle nearby, gently singing romantic songs to her during the night.

After several nights, if the girl's heart had been wooed by the boy's singing, she would go into the jungle and sing in return. At that stage, the two have never met or spoken to each other.[5]

Today the Li courtship custom has changed little in rural areas, but due to the world around them becoming more interconnected, many young Li people find their partners at one of the festivals held each year, such as Sanyesan, where thousands of Li people come together to catch up with their relatives.

Slaves to the spirits

Although most Li women no longer daily wear their traditional dresses, all Li retain their tribal clothing for use at funerals, as it is feared the ghost of the dead person will not be able to find its way to the dwelling place of their ancestors if those attending the funeral are not dressed in correct ethnic attire.

Most Li people today are polytheists, believing in a host of deities which must be placated to assure peace and prosperity in their communities. Offerings and sacrifices are made to various gods, including the spirits believed to inhabit the forces of nature such as mountains, rivers, and even large rocks and trees. A scholar has written this assessment of Li religious beliefs:

> The Li were animists. They were guided in their spiritual affairs by shamans, who through their communications with spirits, deities, and ancestors, functioned as mediators between the physical and supernatural realms. They could harness supernatural power to assure victory in war, hunting, and curing the sick.

But the spiritual favors that were granted to successful mediators could only be achieved through the proper channels: that is, if the spirits of the mountains and ancestors were properly "fed" by the shaman with sacrifices to gain their favor. If, however, the spirits were not properly propitiated, they often turned aggressive and malevolent towards humans and brought sickness or misfortune to the village.[6]

The most powerful god in Li culture is Pathung, who is believed to be good, but he lives in an unknown location that the people can no longer reach. According to the Li worldview,

His agents, devils sent to watch the Li villagers, are ever-present and always live in a nearby cave, in a river, in the jungle, or on a nearby mountain.

At certain times of the year sacrifices to appease the devils are made…. The villages have paid priests, or witchdoctors, who complain to Pathung when local devils get out of hand and spitefully send thunder, lightning, and rain which cause havoc in the fields or when they bring sickness or famine to the people.[7]

More than a century ago, missionary Frank Gilman described the animistic beliefs of the Li people, which bound their communities and caused them to live in fear of the spirit world. He wrote,

They have a strong belief in witchcraft, and their belief in their power to bewitch extends to the Chinese, who will not make a journey into their country without first making a special appeal to the gods for protection. After a hunting party the head of the game is roasted. In the evening the young men gather in the hut of the successful hunter, and after some chanting the roasted head is offered to spirits.[8]

The Li dependence upon the benevolence of the spirit world was also reflected in their practice of headhunting and cannibalism, which is said to have continued into the 1990s. Anthropologist Lars Krutak explained,

A group of Li Christian boys in 1922

The Li concept of sickness was not, as in the West, attributable to bad health. It was a form of punishment, or a disruption of the social order, caused by not fulfilling social duties correctly. Sometimes, sacrifices to the spirits were made in blood and were connected to the practice of headhunting. Shamans not only captured the human blood for use in ritual, but they also prepared the severed heads of slain enemies for burial near the entrance to the village, which was supposed to transform the spirits of the "war-dead" into guardians of the community.[9]

Piercing the darkness

The town of Ledong in southwest Hainan was the base for most early missionary work among the Li people. After a slow start, church membership at Ledong blossomed during the early twentieth century and numbered more than 500 by 1914. The ethnic composition of the Ledong church at the time makes for fascinating reading. The congregation consisted of 240 Li believers, 197 Hakkas, 48 Hainanese, and 24 Mandarin-speaking Han people.[10]

By 1919, the missionaries were encouraged with progress among the Li, with one report noting,

One of our schools is in the Li country, at Baudeng. Two night-schools for little girls are carried on. Including the 110 students of the McCormick School and 40 in the Daughters' School, a total of almost 400 students are under our charge and receiving definite Christian instruction…. Now three women and eight young men form a splendid nucleus for the Church among the Li.[11]

Later, a prominent Li named Li-ek was instrumental in bringing thousands of his people to Christ, although the new converts struggled to live a life totally separated from their old ways. Missionaries worked hard to establish them in the Word of God, but as there were no Scriptures available in the Li language, they often felt the battle was being lost.

By the 1930s many Li people were open to the claims of Christ, and requests were sent for Christians to come and teach them the gospel. All efforts to evangelize and disciple the Li were hindered, however, by the lack of any Scripture in the Li language and

Li-ek, who brought thousands of Li people to Christ

the inability of the Li to understand any of the other languages spoken in Hainan to any great extent.

In 1936, this mission report broke the news that five Li villages had converted to Christianity:

> A party of 19 which included missionaries, an evangelist, a cook, three Li schoolboys and 12 carriers, recently made a two-week trip through that area. They report that not five years ago the number of Christians in the Ha Li area could almost be counted on the fingers of one hand. Now the entire population of five villages worships the Savior.
>
> Not three years ago, these same villages were threatened, and their [Chinese] Bibles, tracts, and hymn books publicly burned. Now the chief of the whole area is an earnest inquirer.
>
> During five days' stay in this region, 87 patients were treated and many inquirers were visited, though none were ready for baptism. For the first time the gospel was taken to the Ha Li tribes themselves. They seemed genuinely interested and asked for more.[12]

Even as the number of professing Li Christians grew, the missionaries realized that the quality of their faith was not maturing at the same rate. Presbyterian missionary Henry Bucher voiced his concerns in 1939:

> At the present stage in our Hainan church there is even a greater need for teaching the Bible to those who are already professing Christians than for bringing larger numbers into churches that already have too few teachers.
>
> The persecution of Christians by one of the Li chiefs is so bad that the Christians have begged me to go out to the country field and see what I can do.... I can talk with him, and we can pray. It is a five-day journey on foot to the area where the trouble is, so I shall have to walk 150 miles, mostly up and down mountains. But it is all part of the Lord's work and there are great rewards.[13]

Heresies infest the Li churches

Throughout the missionary era, the Li received little consistent gospel witness or Bible teaching. Missionaries were handicapped by linguistic, cultural, and geographic barriers. As a result, there are few details about Christian efforts to reach the Li. Many Chinese and foreign believers who tried to share the gospel with them soon became disheartened by the difficulties they faced.

In 1988, a Hong Kong Christian visited a bizarre Li church service at the foot of Wuzhi ("Five Finger") Mountain—which is the largest peak in Hainan, standing 6,125 feet (1,867 meters) above sea level. He reported,

> The chapel had no benches. We learned later that the room was bare of furnishings to provide space for the believers to perform spiritual dances. One such dance is a ritual to heal the sick. When the service begins, believers gathered in the chapel to sing and pray. Then the leader drank a cup of tea, which had been blessed by the Holy Spirit, and sprayed it on the believers. Then they closed their eyes and danced until they became exhausted and fell to the ground.[14]

The reporter then visited another Li church, whose leaders assured him they had abandoned the practice of "spiritual dancing" and "now paid more attention to preaching the Word of God."[15]

Overall, the visitor found the Li fellowships were struggling with disunity, heresy, and lack of Bible knowledge. Summarizing their condition, he gave a mixed opinion:

> On the whole, the Li Christians lack familiarity with the Bible. At each meeting they recite the Lord's Prayer and the Ten Commandments.... Their faith has been handed down from gen-eration to generation. A few elderly and devoted lay believers see to it that they all belong to the Lord. They build up the Lord's house with their own hands and praise the grace of God with

their mouths. Theirs is a simple love of the Lord.... They need help and exposure to other Christian communities in China to grow to maturity in the way of the Lord.[16]

Snippets from Li ministry

The powerful revival that blazed across Hainan in the 1990s drew hundreds of thousands of people into the kingdom of God. At the same time, however, a movement was launched among the Li people to revive their traditional animistic practices, resulting in the rebuilding of temples and ancestral halls. Subsequently, most Li were far less impacted by the revival compared to the Han and other ethnic groups on the island, and relatively few of the more than one million Li people believed the gospel.

In 1990, officials from the Three-Self Patriotic Movement visited Sanya in southern Hainan. At the time, the main registered church in the city was led by a Li pastor, Tan Zhengyi. The church had more than 160 members, with two-thirds being Danjia boat people. Regarding the Li communities in the area,

A group of Christian Li women from the 1930s.
Nearly everyone in their village had believed in Christ

Tan lamented, "Old superstitions practiced by the Li people have a firm hold on them, so there are not many who repent and turn to the Lord. Even among those who do, a good many fall from the faith and do not return."[17]

In 1991, a 50-year-old Chinese Christian man named Lin and his 23-year-old daughter visited Hainan. While there, they were told about a remote community of Li people hidden away in the mountains. The villagers said their forefathers had believed in a God named Jesus, but they no longer knew what that meant. Lin and his daughter were excited by this news and rode bicycles for hours to see if they could bring clarity to the people.

When Lin and his daughter entered the remote Li village, they found the leader and shared Jesus Christ with him, but the man was not interested. Feeling discouraged by their lack of success,

> Lin's daughter whispered, "Father, we have come in the power of our flesh instead of the power of the Spirit. We have not prayed well before we came."
>
> They went back to their hotel and fasted and prayed for three days. Then they went to the village again. This time the leader's attitude was totally different. He received Jesus as his own God, not just the God of his forefathers. He also opened his thatched hut for Lin to start Christian meetings, and eight months later a church of 40 people was established, including a Sunday school for children.[18]

Recruits from the mainland

By the start of the new millennium, several blossoming house church movements in other provinces of China had sent teams of evangelists to reach the Li people in Hainan.

Many of the Chinese missionaries found it difficult to make progress, however. The language barrier was a difficult obstacle to overcome, with many Li people in the mountains speaking little or no Mandarin. In addition, the cultural and religious barriers separating the Li people from the truth of God's grace were larger than many of the visiting Han Christians had anticipated. Still, by persevering and relying on the Holy Spirit, the gospel gradually began to make inroads among the Li.

One young Chinese Christian named Dan moved to Hainan from southwest China. At first, he encountered resistance to his message, but over time God granted a breakthrough. One day, Dan and his wife prayed for a Li woman who had suffered severe back pain for years and was not able to work in the fields. As soon as they finished praying, their prayer was answered.

> The Lord Jesus did a marvelous work. This woman who could not stand upright received an instantaneous healing, believed in the Lord with her whole family, and joined in their harvesting of the crops without any pain. She later testified of her healing in the village, preached the gospel, and led many to the Lord![19]

The same source shared about another key breakthrough in a different Li village:

> A 31-year-old man was so evil that everyone was afraid of him. He would beat up the villagers, steal from them, and even made lunch out of his neighbors' pigs or hens that wandered near his house. No one dared to challenge him. However, after he came to know the Lord, his character changed.
>
> When he lost four of his ten pigs, he said, "Whoever I suspected had stolen my pigs would have received a beating from me. But now that I believe in the Lord, I reckon the loss of my pigs could be due to my past deeds of eating others' pigs. I treat my loss as compensation for my past deeds. From now on, if I see a pig run past my house I will chase it back to its owner. No longer will I help myself to other people's possessions."
>
> Soon after making this declaration, the man lost his other six pigs. He couldn't stand it any longer and wanted to find out who had taken them. A Christian prayed with him, asking the Lord

to intervene. When dawn broke the next morning, the Li man was very excited and exclaimed, "All my pigs have come back. Our God is the true and Living God and He heard our prayers!"[20]

Little Wang beaten to death

When considering the marvelous events that led at least 360,000 people in Hainan coming to Jesus Christ in the 1990s, it's important to know that the revival came at great personal cost to many faithful believers. Some Christians even paid with their very lives.

In 1994, a small group of three Christian men traveled to an unreached Li area to share the gospel, but things did not go to plan. The team consisted of Old Wang, his son Little Wang, and their colleague Cai Wen. A report by a Christian worker in Hainan detailed the dramatic story.

> Old Wang wasn't eager to get home, because he had to face Little Wang's wife, Liang, and her 10-year-old son. He wondered how he would break the news to her that her husband had been murdered

A small group of Li believers in front of their chapel at Zhongcun in 1988
Bridge

by an angry mob of Li people the previous evening. He could still hear the mob's accusations: "The spirits of the mountains rule our land. You Chinese dogs have only been here 500 years and you know nothing. You have stolen our land and now you wish to steal our gods as well. You will pay for this!"

The mob beat the evangelists with sticks and farm implements. A particularly fierce young man continued to beat Little Wang, and when the crowd dispersed, Little Wang didn't move. He had paid the ultimate price. He and his family had only believed in Jesus Christ for five months.[21]

After letting them recover from their injuries for a few weeks, the church decided to send Old Wang and Cai Wen back to the same village to preach again. There were no churches in the entire county, and someone had to take the message of salvation to the Li people. The gathered believers grew silent when Liang spoke up and requested to accompany Old Wang and Cai Wen on their return trip.

The Christians worshipped for hours that day, praying fervently for the trip and for the salvation of the Li. House churches in other parts of the county were also notified to pray and fast for the next three days. A report of their courageous journey said,

The sun had already set when the trio reached their destination, and they slept beside a pigpen outside the village. Whether due to discomfort or busy minds, none of them slept well that night. The next morning they went to the market. Word quickly spread of their return, and as a mob formed some people began to yell threats.

Old Wang felt fear sweep over him.

Suddenly, Liang stepped forward and spoke. "I am the widow of the man you killed less than three weeks ago. My husband is not dead, however, because Jesus Christ has given him eternal life. Now he is living in paradise with God forever. My husband came here to share how you can have that same eternal life. If he was here, he would forgive you for what you did. I forgive you as well. I can forgive you because God has forgiven me. If you would like to hear more about our God, then meet us under the big tree outside the village this evening." A hush came over the crowd and they gradually drifted home.

Old Wang spent the afternoon instructing Liang what to say that night. At sunset, most of the villagers gathered under the big tree to listen to her.

After hearing the Good News of God's way of salvation, many Li people decided to follow Jesus Christ. Old Wang stayed behind to baptize them and to teach them how to serve God, while Cai Wen accompanied Liang on the long bus journey home.

Two months later, Old Wang returned with two leaders and a young man from the new Li church. During the Sunday service, the two leaders brought their greetings and expressed their appreciation.

Then, when the young man stood up to speak, he said, "I am the man who murdered Little Wang. The Lord has graciously forgiven me, and I ask for your forgiveness as well. I, and our entire church, owe an eternal debt of gratitude to Little Wang and Liang for bringing us the message of life. We want to give a monthly love offering to help support Liang and her son. This is the least we can do to show our appreciation."

Several months later, news came from the mountains that the new fellowship had planted another Li church in the same county.[22]

The Li church today

Despite more than a century having passed since the first Li people turned to Christ at Ledong, very few Christians exist among this precious people group today. All five Li tribes remain unreached, with an approximate total of just 1,500 believers among the growing Li population of 1.2 million people.

Today, a paltry one-tenth of one percent of people among each of the five Li subgroups are thought to be followers of Christ, despite increased efforts by house church evangelists who have reached out to the Li in recent decades.

In 2015, the first ever Scripture portions were translated into Li, although the translation doesn't appear to have enjoyed widespread use, and it is unclear which of the five Li dialects was used in the translation. Meanwhile, Christian audio and video resources in Li have been produced and more widely used among the people, including the Li *Jesus* film.

Instead of opening their hearts to the gospel and receiving Jesus as Savior, in recent years many Li communities appear to prefer the ancient polytheistic spirit worship that bound countless past generations of their people.

2000s

House church believers worshipping God with all their hearts
Bibles pour la Chine

The revival that swept across Hainan in the 1990s continued into the new millennium, with joyful pockets of dedicated Christians emerging all over the island in places that had previously been devoid of spiritual light.

Although the main leadership of the Hainan churches continued to come from local Christians, several house church movements from other Chinese provinces also helped stoke the revival by sending evangelists and Bible teachers to Hainan. The Anli house church network in Anhui Province alone had established more than 400 churches throughout the island by the early part of the 21st century.

A church started by a Gospel tract

In 1996 a businessman from central Hainan took a trip to mainland China where someone gave him a Gospel tract. He paid little attention to it, stuffed it in the pocket of his travel bag, and promptly forgot about it.

When he returned home, his wife was unpacking the bag when she discovered the tract. She had never heard of Jesus and knew absolutely nothing about Christianity, but she believed what she read and prayed to receive the Lord.

The woman immediately went to her neighbor and shared her newfound faith. The neighbor also believed, and then the businessman heard the story, and he too gave his life to Christ. They decided the man's wife should travel to Guangzhou and visit an address listed on the back of the tract. She found it was a prominent house church in the city. They gave her Bibles to take back to Hainan and invited her to stay and receive Bible training for two weeks before returning home.

When she arrived back in Hainan, the businessman's wife was chosen to lead the new fellowship, and she shared everything she could remember from the two weeks' Bible training she had received. According to one report,

> When she returned, she was the natural choice as the pastor of this new church. She contacted our workers who traveled down to provide her with further training every week. The church grew to over thirty members in only a couple of months. They had another problem. The house where they met could no longer accommodate growth. They decided to start another church in the next village. That worked well for a couple of months and then both congregations had outgrown their facilities and they had to divide again. This serious problem continues to recur every few months.[1]

As the number of Christians continued to grow because of that one Gospel tract, the believers organized into small groups and were faithful in sharing the gospel with as many lost people as possible. After a while they constructed a cement water tank and held a mass baptismal service for all the new Christians.

Thus, the Lord was glorified in a part of Hainan where the good news had never been proclaimed before—all the result of the life-transforming power of a single Gospel tract.

When God used Mormons

A Christian in Hainan felt impressed to share the gospel with an acquaintance named Dehua. After hearing about Jesus, Dehua showed immediate interest and further meetings were scheduled for her to learn more.

It was carefully explained to Dehua that she would have to count the cost to follow Christ, but after six weeks she was ready to make a firm commitment to the Lord, having become fully convinced that Jesus is the only way to be saved. Dehua recalled how about two years' earlier she had been visited by a Mormon couple who had given her two books—a Bible and a Book of Mormon. She said,

> Every day since then I have read the Bible. I have studied it, taken notes on it, and thought about it. It has become the most important book in my life. However, every time I looked at the Book of Mormon on my shelf I heard a voice saying, "Do not touch that book. It is an evil and dangerous book." As a result, I have never read even one page of it. The only thing I have ever read is the inscription on the inside of the front cover, which says, "Never forget that Jesus loves you and died for your sins."[2]

Dehua became a vibrant Christian and shared Jesus with her unsaved friends, family members, and fellow workers. Many people believed because of her dynamic witness.

Cults make inroads

As the Living God performed a succession of wonderful break-throughs across Hainan during the 1990s and 2000s, it was no surprise that the forces of darkness followed close behind, sowing tares alongside the wheat of God's harvest. Although Western cults like the Mormons and Jehovah's Witnesses were active on the island, far more dangerous to the body of Christ in Hainan was the influence of several destructive Chinese cults.

The most insidious of the cults that preyed on Hainan was undoubtedly the Eastern Lightning, a wicked group based in central China that believes Jesus Christ has returned to the earth as a Chinese woman. They frequently use violence against Christians who resist them, and cult members have murdered many people across China. After gaining millions of members in mainland China, Eastern Lightning members arrived in Hainan.

Not content with just trying to win the general population to their false religion, the Eastern Lightning specifically targeted new believers in both Three-Self and unregistered churches. In Hainan, the cult also boldly targeted Western Christians who were serving on the island as undercover missionaries. One foreign couple, who taught at a school for five years, shared some of the subtle ways the cult targeted new believers in their town:

Three months ago our nanny, who was a strong believer with a long-term illness, was sucked in by the cult. A man posing as a doctor claimed he could heal her, but she would need to come to his home for several days of treatment. We warned her not to go, but she went anyway. When she returned, she was a completely different woman. She was drugged while there, being given a "tonic" to drink twice a day.

Our nanny had previously been a cheerful person who encouraged people to follow Jesus and read the Bible, but now she appeared exhausted and depressed. Finally, the local house church leaders told us she had joined the Eastern Lightning and was traveling around the island converting people to the cult.

One Sunday, about a dozen of our Christian students were at their local house church meeting when a couple handed out little books to all the students, saying they needed to be careful about the Eastern Lightning, and that the book would help protect them.

The students showed us the books. They were all in Chinese, except a tiny inscription on the last page that said the books were published by "Lightning from the East"! There was a paragraph at the start of the book, and another at the end, warning against the cult, but the rest of the book was packed full of their poisonous teachings, with a selection of Bible verses thrown in to deceive readers. Obviously, these books create confusion in the minds of immature believers. Satan is using this cult to destroy the faith of many children of God.[3]

Training the next generation

During many revivals in history—when God powerfully shakes a nation to its core and multitudes of people enter His kingdom in a short period of time—the church begins to think about how to preserve the harvest, lest it be lost to decay over time.

Although aggressive evangelism and church planting continued in Hainan throughout the 2000s and to the present time, churches also thought about how they could best establish the hundreds of thousands of new converts in the faith.

Many decided that training children in the Word of God was a crucial need, especially as all education in China is strictly based on atheism and Marxist-Leninist ideology. As most children only hear God being mentioned at school and in society when he is mocked, the body of Christ countered this influence by establishing excellent discipleship programs for children.

To consolidate gains from the revival, the Hainan church focused on training children in the 2000s
CCI

A key part of the curriculum was a DVD series with 15 hours of excellent teaching, which trained Sunday school teachers how to effectively reach children and nurture them in the faith.

In Communist China the authorities especially hate it when Christians minister to children, and severe consequences often follow. The intensity of the reaction reveals the spiritual importance of this vital outreach, in a country where the government believes they control the thoughts and actions of all children, and outside influences are not tolerated.

In 2006, this report from a mission organization told of a children's training course in Hainan, and the extreme battle that ensued when the teachers traveled from mainland China:

> Over the years more than 100,000 children's workers have been trained throughout China through Sister Hui's Sunday school

curriculum. Due to the tremendous need for children's workers, she is constantly in demand for traveling and ministering.

Recently, Sister Hui and her coworkers traveled to Hainan to conduct training. Potential children's workers, eager to be trained, gathered at different locations.

As Sister Hui and her team were seated by their departure gate at a major Chinese airport waiting to fly to Hainan, she went to check on when their flight would board and asked her colleagues to watch her briefcase. When she returned moments later, she was surprised to find her briefcase missing, probably stolen. In it were important documents and training materials she needed to conduct the course, and her digital camera that contained images from other recent training sessions.

The team decided to continue to their destination and were taken to a rural area of Hainan where expectant believers awaited them. Just before the training was scheduled to begin the next morning, however, sixteen Public Security officers showed up in the village to monitor what was going on. The house church leaders quickly changed the location for the training to another village which they felt would be safer.

After the first three-hour training session was completed, Sister Hui and the believers sat down for a meal together when a local rushed in to say they needed to leave immediately as the police had arrived at the outskirts of the village.

After hiding Sister Hui and her coworkers for several hours, the house church leaders decided to relocate the meetings again. To reach the new village they rode on the back of motorcycles along bumpy dirt roads, but when they turned a corner they saw in the distance that three police cars were blocking the way. The motorcycle drivers used their local knowledge to creatively avoid the blockade, riding through a forest until they reached their destination.

After the tense training course had finally been completed, the team again faced great danger when they tried to leave the area, with all roads and bridges teeming with armed officers.

After napping for a few hours, the ministry team was awakened and told that many of the local Christians were being arrested. They decided to surrender to the police to prevent more believers from being persecuted. They calmly walked up to a roadblock where three police cars and ten officers were stationed and said, "We are the ones you are looking for."[4]

The result was that they were taken to a local police station and interrogated, but when asked to hand over all their Christian materials, they could honestly reply they had none, except for one Bible. Sister Hui began to realize the wisdom of God behind her briefcase going missing, as it contained a huge amount of incriminating evidence and materials that would have landed her in prison for years.

Because the authorities could not find evidence to prosecute them, Sister Hui and her team were allowed to go. They departed Hainan with a new appreciation of the level of spiritual warfare required there, and a deep realization that Satan would not stand by and let the mighty revival continue to spread without a massive struggle.

The battle of the researchers

For decades, many believers around the world have been confused by disparate information about the church in China. Some Christian organizations insist there is a great famine of Bibles in the country, while others claim there is no shortage at all. Similarly, some prominent mission leaders claim there is little or no persecution of Christians in China today, while other ministries have as their core activity the careful documentation of persecution against the church.

Another source of confusion has been the varying estimates of the size of the church in China. A disagreement involving

Hainan occurred in the late 1990s and early 2000s, after news emerged of the tremendous spiritual awakening on the island.

By the start of the new millennium, several dependable workers in Hainan had conducted island-wide surveys that found the number of house church Christians had rapidly increased to between 250,000 and 360,000 believers.

One of the key researchers and proponents of this higher figure was a highly-respected resident Southern Baptist missionary. He had lived in Hainan since the start of the revival and had personally witnessed it up close. His research was accepted by other mission organizations and by Patrick Johnstone, the compiler of the authoritative *Operation World*. In the 2001 edition of the book, Johnstone listed a figure of 334,100 Evangelical Christians in Hainan.[5]

Some of the hundreds of thousands of Hainan
Christians at the start of the 21st century
RCMI

Tony Lambert, a now-retired British researcher and author associated with the Overseas Missionary Fellowship, had long been recognized as a researcher who displayed abundant caution against some of the higher estimates of Christians in China. Lambert's critics over the years, however, frequently lamented his tendency to side with Three-Self Church estimates, while he appeared to be poorly connected to house church networks and so was ignorant of much of the spectacular revival that had occurred throughout China.

In 1999, Lambert wrote a book that provided a snapshot of Christianity in each province of China. When summarizing Hainan, he wrote, "Hainan has at least 37,000 Christians.... Wanning County on the east coast may have 10,000 believers, 90 percent of whom meet in independent house churches.... House churches in Hainan are numerous but appear to be split with rivalries between leaders."[6]

Two sets of research therefore painted starkly divergent views on the size of the Hainan church, with Lambert sticking with the long-published official figure of just 37,000 believers on the island,[7] despite well-connected resident Christians detailing a church approximately ten times that size.

When he was put in touch with the Baptist missionary in Hainan, Lambert was told of the tremendous growth occurring on the island, but he stubbornly refused to believe it. Lambert wrote, "In the south, Sanya and inland, there doesn't seem to be a lot of house churches."[8] In response, the missionary said, "That's simply ridiculous. In Sanya County there are churches in virtually every fishing village. There are also plenty of inland churches."[9]

Researchers often struggle to keep up with the rapid pace of change in China, and the old Three-Self figure of 37,000 Christians in Hainan, which Lambert was still using in 2003, is quoted by some sources even today. That figure is woefully out of date and completely ignores the mighty revival that took place on the island.

Despite first-hand evidence to the contrary, Lambert doubled down on his low estimate, restating that none of his sources in Hainan believed it possible for there to be more than 50,000 believers on the island. The missionary responded with more details of the move of God, writing, "One independent source here has claimed 250,000 believers. Another Singaporean researcher gives a number of 360,000. This year I had a friend go and do on-site verification in one part of the island of 78,500 Christians, so I am absolutely, positively sure the number is at least that high."[10]

When I spoke with a key Christian in Hainan who was heavily involved with the house church revival, I repeated Lambert's claim that there were just 37,000 Christians on the island. In response, the man laughed out loud and said, "That is stupid! I have personally met at least 150,000 believers."[11]

In April 2003, Lambert published a new "Survey of the Chinese Church." Those hoping to see a correction of his statistics were dismayed, however, with Lambert's Hainan summary stating, "The total number of believers was 37,000 according to a TSPM estimate, but reliable house church estimates in 2002 also put the number at not above 50,000. Reports that there are over 300,000 believers on the island have been denied as not credible by both local house church evangelists and TSPM pastors."[12]

Finally, when asked if he had ever personally visited Hainan Island, Tony Lambert refused to answer. Instead, he stubbornly refused to adjust his position being presented with clear evidence that his research was faulty and his credibility as a fair-minded researcher was questioned.

As the first decade of the 21st century drew to a close, the church in Hainan had been through many battles but had emerged triumphant, though it was battered and bruised as the

Hainan authorities implemented orders from Beijing to crush the Christian revival. The Communist Party had plans to turn Hainan into a high-class resort destination and a center for international investment, and the last thing they wanted was for the island to become a hub of Christianity.

Despite the province-wide crackdown designed to stop the spread of the gospel, the number of believers in Hainan continued to grow during the 2000s, though at a slightly slower rate compared to the 1990s.

The influential mission book *Operation World* had estimated a total of 334,100 Evangelical Christians in Hainan in its 2001 edition.[13] By the end of the decade, however, its new estimate reflected the continued growth of the church in Hainan, with a figure of 533,900 Evangelical believers published in the 2010 edition of the book.[14]

Letters from Hainan

2001

All the believers here are farmers. As some are poorly educated, they never read the Bible. They totally abide by the teaching of those brothers who lead them. They were told that Jesus' Name has been changed to Christ and that people should put their trust in Christ instead of Jesus. All the contents of their prayers are planned by their leaders. They advocate confessing one's own sins but discourage praying for other people or for other matters. Moreover, these leaders are strongly convinced that other than themselves, all people are faulty, and so they do not accept other people's opinions.[15]

Previously, all the inhabitants of our island went to a city hospital to treat their illnesses. Many people were healed after some evangelists prayed for them. As a result the gospel spread, and now one-tenth of the population have found faith in Christ.[16]

In our village, most of the people are idolaters. They are very stubborn and pay no attention to the goodness of God or His salvation. They even mock our faith, saying that no men will marry us Christian women. Our families also threaten to turn us out of the house if we insist on going to Sunday church services. Although one sister knew this was a trap of Satan, she was defeated and now I go to Sunday service alone. Thank the Lord for His love. My faith is indeed growing in Him.[17]

2002

In the northern part of the island, some church leaders use oppressive ways to manipulate their flocks. They forbid believers to read the accepted version of the Bible and only allow them to read the version "modified" by them, which has had the Book of Revelation deleted and the doctrine of "justification by faith in Christ" in the book of Romans changed to "justification by deeds."[18]

2003

A church here has adopted some Old Testament practices. They have partitioned their church into two parts—the Holy Place and the Most Holy Place. No one in the congregation is allowed to enter the Most Holy Place, not even for janitorial purposes. They regard their pastor as if he were a high priest in the Old Testament. They assume that everything he handles has a special spiritual anointing, and that even a cup of drinking water can be transformed into a panacea for healing and casting out demons. Henceforth, the believers ask their pastor to intercede for them in all matters.[19]

2004

I am a very ordinary person, but our local authorities have labeled me "dangerous" because I preach the gospel. They have placed me under surveillance, but recently we established a new church of 20 people, and it was placed under my care. So far in the last ten years we have started 21 churches, but we have been constantly attacked by Satan. Please pray for us![20]

When I was 11 years old my parents divorced, which brought deep sadness into my life for years. Then one night I had a vivid dream. I saw the Lord Jesus Christ Himself, who told me that I am His child and one day I would serve Him. I never forgot His promise, and I am now aged 19 and I serve the Lord as a Sunday school teacher. Jesus also used the hard times in my life to fulfill a good purpose. Because of the pain of those difficult times, I found a deep relationship with the Lord. I'm still young, but God has called me to do this Sunday school teacher's work and I want to serve Him my whole life until my hair turns gray.[21]

2005

One church here woke up to the need to do children's ministry after a seven-year-old Christian girl was kidnapped. The whole church cried out in prayer for God's intervention. She was taken to a place where children have their organs harvested and sold by evil people. The little girl was bound to a pole in the center of a room where the corpses of dead children lay on the floor. She prayed "Jesus, please help me and send someone to rescue me!" God heard her prayer after three days and sent an old Christian lady to cut her ropes and take her back home.[22]

2006

In our church we have a 12-year-old boy who had a wound on his leg. His mother wasn't concerned and thought he had picked up a knock while playing with his friends. When his leg became increasingly painful, the mother took her son to see a doctor. He was diagnosed with cancer and sent to the hospital. Despite their treatment, the boy's condition did not improve and he was in terrible pain.

One day a Sunday school teacher came to the hospital and stopped by the boy's bed. She told him about Jesus and prayed for him. Before she left, she gave him a Bible story book and asked him to read it carefully every day. The boy read it again and again and prayed the salvation prayer printed on the last page. His mother was surprised when she saw that even though her son was in severe pain, he was peaceful and even happy. He told his mother, "I don't feel pain anymore, because when Jesus was dying on the cross for my sins, His pain was much worse."

Finally the day came when God's angel came to take the boy home to heaven, where he could see Jesus face to face and suffer no more pain or tears. On the day of the funeral, his mother said, "I want to put his Bible story book in his arms. It was so dear to him and made him happy, and we too should believe in Jesus."[23]

2010s and 2020s

A new kind of persecution

In the 2010s, as the government aggressively tried to transform Hainan into "China's Hawaii," it was inevitable that commercialism would clash with the growth of Christianity. The greedy authorities created disputes over church land and buildings to persecute Christians. The following example took place on the morning of August 13, 2013.

> A number of Christians in Lingao town, Lincheng County, were violently beaten by urban management officers when they tried

Two of the Christian women severely beaten by authorities in Hainan when their church building was sold to developers
China Aid

to prevent construction at a building site. A Christian church was originally intended to be built at the site; however, the site was later secretly sold to developers by the local government.

Several children and elderly were injured during the attack, and two women who were protesting the construction are in a coma because of the retaliation.[1]

In other parts of the province, both registered Three-Self and unregistered house church congregations, with legally purchased land and buildings, suddenly had their titles voided by corrupt officials. Elsewhere, congregations that met in rented facilities had their leases cancelled, as the Hainan government did all they could to prevent the continued rise of Christianity.

The summer of 2013 saw the launch of many actions against house churches in southern Hainan, with Sanya bearing the brunt of government action. Initially there was hope that the newly-appointed President of China, Xi Jinping, would bring a new era of freedom for Christians in Hainan, but those hopes were quickly snuffed out. One report on the trouble in Sanya said,

> The Chinese government has shut down at least a dozen house churches in the southern province of Hainan in recent weeks and many others have been threatened with closure, a sign that little has changed under the new leadership of Xi Jinping.
>
> On May 26, while the Sanya Hosanna Church was holding a morning worship service, seven or eight people from the Religious Affairs Bureau and the neighborhood committee...told the believers to go to the city's registered religious meeting sites, warning that if the believers met again the next week the officials would take measures and would hold the believers accountable for the consequences. The committee also exerted pressure on the landlord to stop renting the meeting site to the church and gave them 15 days' notice to move out....
>
> Also on May 26, three other Sanya house congregations— Elim Church, Bethel Church, and Xinju Church—faced the same

kind of persecution. Two weeks earlier, Sanya's Mengai Church, Hexing Church, and three other house churches were also shut down. A church in Haikou has faced the same situation, and

A modern Three-Self church in Hainan
RCMI

seven or eight other churches have been shut down, as have some churches in Baoting County.[2]

Revival spreads to the registered church

The reputation of the Three-Self Church in Hainan was deservedly at a very low ebb in the 1980s and 1990s, as many of its leaders proved to be little more than atheist puppets and mouthpieces of the Communist Party.

By the start of the new millennium, however, the mighty revival that was sweeping the house churches in Hainan began to overflow into the registered churches. Leaders who remained loyal to the government's anti-religious policies soon found themselves powerless to stop the surge, as the Holy Spirit broke down the walls and the Three-Self Patriotic Movement also found themselves caught up in the flood of heaven-sent revival.

Those who had served Christ in Hainan during the 1980s and 1990s never imagined the time would come when the Holy Spirit would have free reign in the registered churches on the island. Indeed, in the 1990s the registered churches were in dire spiritual condition, with the most noteworthy incidents occurring when faithful preachers of the gospel were dragged from the pulpit and imprisoned by corrupt Three-Self leaders.

The Living God, however, is never slow to meet a challenge head-on, and the people found His presence irresistible. For a time, some of the government-appointed church leaders tried to stem the flow, but most gave up as they saw the futility of trying to stop a move of God.

For many years the number of Three-Self Church members in Hainan was officially stuck at 37,000, but by the 2020s the government-approved churches on the island contained an estimated 170,000 believers,[3] who worshipped and proclaimed the gospel with relative freedom compared to previous decades.

Numerous Bible schools had sprung up to train a new generation of evangelists and church leaders. The Lord Jesus Christ had decided to visit Hainan, and wherever He found willing hearts He touched and transformed them—including within the confines of the government-approved churches.

In "Table 2: All Christians in Hainan" found in this book's appendix, we have acknowledged the continued growth of the church in Hainan in recent years, and estimate there are presently 615,000 Evangelical Christians on the island, divided between 170,000 members of registered churches, and 445,000 believers who worship in unregistered house church meetings.

While Christians should praise God for the great things He has done among the churches of Hainan during the past 20 years, it is sobering to realize that 562,000 Evangelical Christians represents less than six percent of the island's population.

Students at a Three-Self Bible school in Hainan in the mid-2010s
RCMI

Xi Jinping's reign of terror

After President Xi Jinping quietly came to power in 2013, he swiftly removed any dissenting voices from the government, replacing them with officials who would only submit to his autocratic rule. According to several of his speeches, a key part of his plan was to create an atheistic utopia in China, leading ultimately to the elimination of all religion.

For China's many tens of millions of house church Christians, the turning point in their freedoms came in 2016 at a little-known meeting, when a group of senior house church leaders in China were summoned to Beijing for a secret audience with Xi.

In that meeting, the Chinese president bluntly informed the church leaders that his patience had run out, and they had six months to register their networks of churches under the authority of the Religious Affairs Bureau, or they would face severe consequences.

A few months later, a large gathering of house church leaders from multiple networks took place at a hotel on Hainan Island. In that meeting, some of the elderly men who had met with Xi Jinping shared the content of their discussions and the grave threat that Xi issued. Some advised it was time for their churches to register, that a new era had dawned in China, and the church should work with the government instead of being in constant conflict with them.

In response, some of the younger church leaders launched passionate rebuttals of that advice, with one saying,

> You older brothers have suffered much for the gospel in your generation. You carried the flame and spent years in prison and on the run. You taught us not to compromise, but that only Jesus Christ can be Head of the Church, not an atheistic political party.
>
> Shame on you! You can register your churches with the government if you like, but we will never compromise! We will never

submit to a God-hating structure! We don't care what consequences our actions bring. We are willing to suffer and die for the Lord and for His Church.[4]

Like clockwork, exactly six months after President Xi Jinping issued his threat, house churches across China began to experience a new wave of persecution, which intensified with each passing month and each new draft of anti-religious laws that were introduced.

Although the normal forms of persecution continued against Hainan's Christians with arrests, imprisonments, and the closure of church buildings, an even greater form of persecution affected believers on a personal level, with countless followers of Jesus subjected to state-sanctioned harassment and discrimination. This included Christian children being expelled from schools and blocked from attending university, believers losing their jobs, and elderly followers of Christ having their pensions and health care revoked if they refused to renounce their faith.

During Xi's years in power, almost all foreign Christians have been expelled from China, and foreign investment in Hainan has taken a massive hit, exacerbated by Xi's fanatical "zero covid" policies, which essentially shut down the island's tourist industry for extended periods between 2020 and 2022.

The Future of the Church in Hainan

The island God remembered

The history of Christianity in Hainan is markedly different from most other parts of China. Whereas other provinces have detailed and rich histories of the gospel as it was established and prospered over the decades, Hainan was comparatively neglected during the missionary era, despite the efforts of the mysterious Danish sea captain Carl Jeremiassen, and the godly witness of a succession of Presbyterian missionaries including Frank Gilman, Henry McCandliss, and Margaret Moninger. These pioneers served faithfully and well, laying a strong template for future generations to emulate of hard work, perseverance, and the faithful application of God's word.

A small remnant of believers remained in Hainan while the Communists tried to completely snuff out the light of the gospel from the 1950s to 1970s. The remnant finally emerged—battered and bruised, but secure in the hands of God—and during the 1980s the church rose again as the atmosphere in China began to thaw.

Although Hainan is the smallest of China's provinces, God did not forget it, and in the 1990s a remarkable and far-reaching revival swept the island, saving hundreds of thousands of people and impacting almost every segment of society.

The revival continued into the new millennium, and the Name of Jesus Christ is still being exalted and proclaimed in Hainan today, with sinners finding forgiveness at the foot of the cross.

In recent years, the Christians in Hainan have faced new challenges as they evolve to meet the changing needs of Christians in their midst, while at the same time they have not stopped preaching the gospel to the lost.

The severe nationwide crackdown against Christianity, launched by President Xi Jinping in 2017, has also affected believers in Hainan, with intense pressure being placed on church leaders to disband their meetings. Many have been arrested, and news from Hainan has dried up as Christians avoid giving reports from the island.

In 2020, an article in the Hong Kong-based *South China Morning Post* reported that foreign teachers in Hainan were placed under severe restrictions to stop sharing their faith with students, either in the classroom or in private. The article said,

> New foreign hires will have to complete 20 hours of political indoctrination covering China's development, laws, professional ethics, and education policies. Authorities have also proposed a national social credit system to score foreign teachers on what they do and say—inside and outside the classroom.
>
> The public security department in the southern province of Hainan has gone so far as to offer rewards of up to 100,000 Yuan ($14,600) for tip-offs leading to the arrest of foreigners who "engage in religious activities without permission." This includes teaching religion, evangelizing, and networking.[1]

The first Christians in the Book of Acts experienced tremendous revival, miracles, and unprecedented growth, but the next generation of believers needed to be established in the faith, so the focus shifted to church leadership and discipleship, as seen by the different emphasis in the Apostle Paul's later letters.

Likewise, the church in Hainan rode the exciting waves of revival in the 1990s and early 2000s, but now the focus has shifted from not only gathering in the harvest, but in putting a structure in place that will provide a sound theological foundation, assuring the harvest doesn't go to waste.

In recent years many Bible schools and house church training centers have emerged throughout the island, and God has raised up gifted Bible teachers, theologians, and writers, whose work complements the many evangelists and church planters who continue to seek out people in Hainan who have yet to hear of Jesus Christ.

As readers of this book will realize, the church in Hainan was a very modest size until the revival of the 1990s swept hundreds of thousands of people into the kingdom of God. As the table and graphs in the following pages show, today more than 600,000 Christians live in Hainan—most of whom are members of Evangelical house church movements.

As we reach the end of our look at the wonderful things God has done in Hainan, may we give thanks to the Lord Jesus Christ, whose blood has purchased men for God from every tribe, people group, language, and nation on Hainan Island.

At the time of this book's publication, Hainan's Christians were experiencing the most severe persecution in their history—with the possible exception of the Cultural Revolution from 1966 to 1976. With them, we long for the day when God shall draw a line in the sand and say, "Enough" to those dictating the harsh anti-Christ policies. Then, we confidently believe, the spiritual foundation of the Hainan church, so lovingly laid by both the early missionaries and during the great revival of the last few decades, will prove its mettle having withstood the heat of the furnace, and the church will come out refined, more committed to Christ and His Word, and better-placed than before to glorify God among the people of Hainan.

Appendix

---•●•---

Table 1. Evangelical Christians in Hainan (1869–2023)

(Includes both Three-Self and house churches)

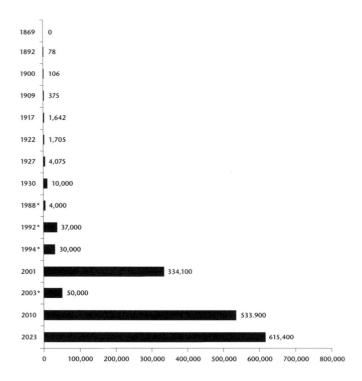

Sources for Table 1.

0	(1869)
78	(1892 – Gilman, *The Isle of Palms*)
106	(1900 – Brown, *Earthen Vessels and Transcendent Power*)
375	(1909 – Gilman, *The Isle of Palms*)
1,642	(1917 – Gilman, *The Isle of Palms*)
1,705	(1922 – Stauffer, *The Christian Occupation of China*)
4,075	(1927 – Brown, *Earthen Vessels and Transcendent Power*)
10,000	(1930 – *Bridge*, January–February 1988)
4,000*	(1988 – *Bridge*, January–February 1988)
37,000*	(1992 – *Bridge*, May 1992)
30,000*	(1994 – Amity News Service, 1994)
50,000*	(2003 – Global Chinese Ministries, April 2003)
334,100	(2001 – Johnstone & Mandryk, *Operation World*)
533,900	(2010 – Mandryk, *Operation World*)
615,400	(2023 – Hattaway, *The China Chronicles*)

* These sources may only refer to registered church estimates. TSPM figures typically only count adult baptized members.

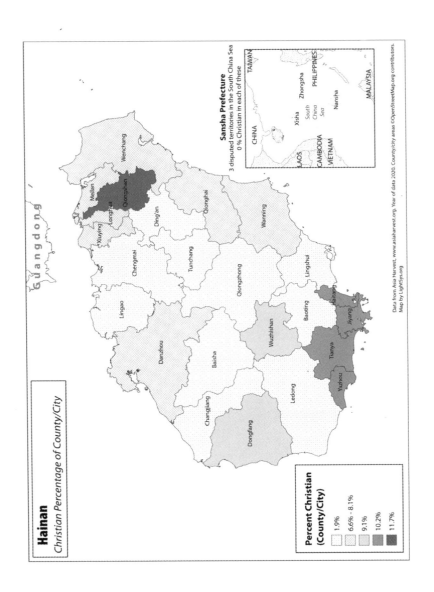

Table 2. All Christians in Hainan

| Hainan 海南 | | POPULATION | | | | | CHRISTIANS | | | | | | Total Christians | |
Location		Census 2000	Census 2010	Growth	Growth (percent)	Estimate 2020	Evangelicals TSPM	Evangelicals House church	TOTAL Evangelicals	Catholics CPA	Catholics House church	TOTAL Catholics	TOTAL	Percent of 2020 population
Danzhou Prefecture	儋州市	835,465	932,356	96,891	11.60%	1,029,247	18,526	48,169	66,695	453	906	1,359	68,054	6.61%
Danzhou City	儋州市	835,465	932,356	96,891	11.60%	1,029,247	18,526	48,169	66,695	453	906	1,359	68,054	6.61%
Haikou Prefecture	海口市	1,508,341	2,046,170	468,896	31.09%	2,515,066	60,131	156,341	216,472	1,107	2,213	3,320	219,792	8.74%
Longhua District	龙华区	317,508	593,018	275,510	86.77%	868,528	19,108	49,680	68,787	382	764	1,146	69,934	8.05%
Meilan District	美兰区	623,653	623,653	0	0.00%	623,653	13,720	35,673	49,393	274	549	823	50,217	8.05%
Qiongshan District	琼山区	479,958	479,958	0	0.00%	479,958	15,359	39,933	55,291	211	422	634	55,925	11.65%
Xiuying District	秀英区	156,155	349,541	193,386	123.84%	542,927	11,944	31,055	43,000	239	478	717	43,716	8.05%
Sansha Prefecture (disputed territories in the South China Sea)	三沙市	517	444	-73	-14.12%	371	0	0	0	0	0	0	0	0.00%
Nansha (Spratly Islands)	南沙群岛	0	0	0	0.00%	0	0	0	0	0	0	0	0	
Xisha (Paracel Islands)	西沙群岛	517	444	-73	-14.12%	371	0	0	0	0	0	0	0	
Zhongsha (Macclesfield Bank)	中沙群岛的岛礁及其海域	0	0	0	0.00%	0	0	0	0	0	0	0	0	
Sanya Prefecture	三亚市	482,296	685,408	0	0.00%	685,408	19,191	49,898	69,089	302	603	905	69,994	10.21%
Haitang District	海棠区	68,878	68,878	0	0.00%	68,878	1,929	5,014	6,943	30	61	91	7,034	10.21%
Jiyang District	吉阳区	257,469	257,469	0	0.00%	257,469	7,209	18,744	25,953	113	227	340	26,293	10.21%
Tianya District	天涯区	269,546	269,546	0	0.00%	269,546	7,547	19,623	27,170	119	237	356	27,526	10.21%
Yazhou District	崖州区	89,515	89,515	0	0.00%	89,515	2,506	6,517	9,023	39	79	118	9,141	10.21%

Table of All Christians in Hainan

Hainan 海南		POPULATION					CHRISTIANS							Total Christians	
							Evangelicals			Catholics					
Location	Counties and Cities directly administered by Hainan 海南省省直辖县级行政区划	Census 2000	Census 2010	Growth	Growth (percent)	Estimate 2020	TSPM	House church	TOTAL Evangelicals	CPA	House church	TOTAL Catholics	TOTAL	TOTAL	Percent of 2020 population
Baisha County	白沙黎族自治县	164,494	167,918	3,424	2.08%	171,342	857	2,227	3,084	75	151	226	3,310		1.93%
Baoting County	保亭黎族苗族自治县	139,506	146,684	7,178	5.15%	153,862	769	2,000	2,770	68	135	203	2,973		1.93%
Changjiang County	昌江黎族自治县	219,502	223,839	4,337	1.98%	228,176	1,141	2,966	4,107	100	201	301	4,408		1.93%
Chengmai County	澄迈县	434,598	467,161	32,563	7.49%	499,724	4,997	12,993	17,990	220	440	660	18,650		3.73%
Ding'an County	定安县	279,335	284,614	5,279	1.89%	289,893	1,449	3,769	5,218	128	255	383	5,601		1.93%
Dongfang City	东方市	358,318	408,309	49,991	13.95%	458,300	11,458	29,790	41,247	202	403	605	41,852		9.13%
Ledong County	乐东黎族自治县	447,382	458,875	11,493	2.57%	470,368	2,352	6,115	8,467	207	414	621	9,088		1.93%
Lingao County	临高县	389,734	427,873	38,139	9.79%	466,012	6,990	18,174	25,165	205	410	615	25,780		5.53%
Lingshui County	陵水黎族自治县	303,272	320,468	17,196	5.67%	337,664	1,688	4,390	6,078	149	297	446	6,524		1.93%
Qionghai City	琼海市	449,845	483,217	33,372	7.42%	516,589	11,365	29,549	40,914	227	455	682	41,596		8.05%
Qiongzhong County	琼中黎族苗族自治县	171,598	174,076	2,478	1.44%	176,554	883	2,295	3,178	78	155	233	3,411		1.93%
Tunchang County	屯昌县	251,121	256,931	5,810	2.31%	262,741	1,314	3,416	4,729	116	231	347	5,076		1.93%
Wanning City	万宁市	513,604	545,597	31,993	6.23%	577,590	12,707	33,038	45,745	254	508	762	46,508		8.05%
Wenchang City	文昌市	509,271	537,426	28,155	5.53%	565,581	12,443	32,351	44,794	249	498	747	45,541		8.05%
Wuzhishan City	五指山市	100,836	104,119	3,283	3.26%	107,402	2,685	6,981	9,666	47	95	142	9,808		9.13%
Totals		4,732,416	5,007,107	274,691	5.80%	5,281,798	73,098	190,054	263,152	2,324	4,648	6,972	270,124		5.11%
		7,559,035	8,671,485	1,112,450	14.72%	9,783,935	170,947	444,461	615,408	4,185	8,370	12,555	627,963		6.42%

Table 3. People Groups in Hainan

People Group	Official Nationality	Primary Language	Primary Religion	Population (all of China) 2020	All Christians		Evangelicals	
Cun	Han	Cun	Animism	97,000	4,000	4.1%	4,000	4.1%
Fuma	Han	Foma	No Religion	1,100	29	2.6%	26	2.3%
Hakka, Hainan Island	Han	Chinese, Hakka	Daoism	2,400	108	4.5%	96	4.0%
Han Chinese, Hainanese	Han	Chinese, Min Nan	No Religion	5,855,000	526,950	9.0%	521,095	8.9%
Indonesian	Han	Indonesian	Christianity	11,000	5,610	51.0%	5,000	45.5%
Li, Bendi	Li	Hlai	Animism	80,000	80	0.1%	80	0.1%
Li, Ha	Li	Hlai	Animism	701,000	1,402	0.2%	771	0.1%
Li, Jiamao	Li	Jiamao	Animism	94,000	188	0.2%	66	0.1%
Li, Meifu	Li	Hlai	Animism	54,000	54	0.1%	16	0.0%
Li, Qi	Li	Hlai	Animism	320,000	640	0.2%	448	0.1%
Lingao	Han	Lingao	Animism	686,000	28,812	4.2%	27,440	4.0%
Utsat	Hui	Tsat	Islam	8,400	0	0.0%	0	0.0%
Vietnamese	Han	Viet	No Religion	23,000	690	3.0%	35	0.2%
Totals				**7,932,900**	**568,563**	**7.2%**	**559,072**	**7.0%**

Groups primarily located in Hainan. Latest stats from www.joshuaproject.net

Researching Christians in China

When Marco Polo made his famous journey to "the Orient" 750 years ago, he documented the existence of Nestorian churches and monasteries in various places, to the fascination of people in Europe.

Since I started traveling to China in the 1980s, I have found that believers around the world are still eager to know how many Christians there are in China. Many people are aware that God has done a remarkable work in this hugely populous country, but little research has been done to put a figure on the phenomenon. In recent decades, wildly divergent estimates have been published, ranging from 20 million to 230 million. An example of this divergence is discussed in the 2000s chapter of this book under the subheading "The battle of the researchers."

Methodology

In the following table, I provide estimates of the number of Christians in Hainan. Full tables of the other provinces of China can be found at the Asia Harvest website. (See "The Church in China" link under the Resources tab at www.asiaharvest.org.) My survey provides figures for Christians of every description, arranged in four main categories: the Three-Self Patriotic Movement, the Evangelical house churches, the Catholic Patriotic Association, and the Catholic house churches. I have supplied statistics for all 2,800 cities and counties within every province, municipality, and autonomous region of China.

The information was gathered from a wide variety of sources. More than 2,000 published sources have been noted in the tables published online, including a multitude of books, journals, magazine articles, and reports that I have accumulated meticulously over many years. I have also conducted hundreds of hours of interviews with key house church leaders from many different branches of God's work throughout China.

In compiling the data, I began with this assumption: that in any given place in the country there are no Christians at all, until I have a figure from a documented source or can make an intelligent estimate based on information gathered from Christian leaders in China. I wanted to put aside all personal bias, input all the information I found, and see what the totals came to.

A note about security

None of the information provided in these tables is new to the Chinese government. Beijing has clearly already thoroughly researched the spread of Christianity throughout the country, as shown by the Director of the Religious Affairs Bureau Ye Xiaowen's 2006 announcement that there were then 130 million Christians in China.[1] In December 2009, the national newspaper *China Daily* interviewed scholar Liu Peng who had spent years researching religion for the Chinese Academy of Social Sciences. Liu claimed the "house churches have at least 50 million followers nationwide."[2] His figure at the time was consistent with my research.

After consulting various house church leaders in China, all of them were content that this information should be published, as long as the survey focused on statistics and avoided specific information such as the names and locations of Christian leaders, as it does.

The Chinese church in perspective

All discussion of how many Christians there are in China should be tempered by the realization that more than 90 percent of its present population face a Christ-less eternity. Hundreds of millions of individuals have yet to hear the gospel. House church leaders in China have told me how ashamed and burdened they feel that so many of their countrymen and women do not yet know Jesus Christ. This burden motivates them to do whatever it takes to preach the gospel among every ethnic group and in every city, town, and village—to every individual—in China, and to do whatever necessary to see Christ exalted throughout the land.

May we humbly give thanks to the Living God for the great things He has done in China. We are privileged to live in a remarkable time in human history, like in the days prophesied by the prophet Habakkuk:

> Look at the nations and watch—
>   and be utterly amazed.
> For I am going to do something in your days
>   that you would not believe, even if you were told. (Hab. 1:5)

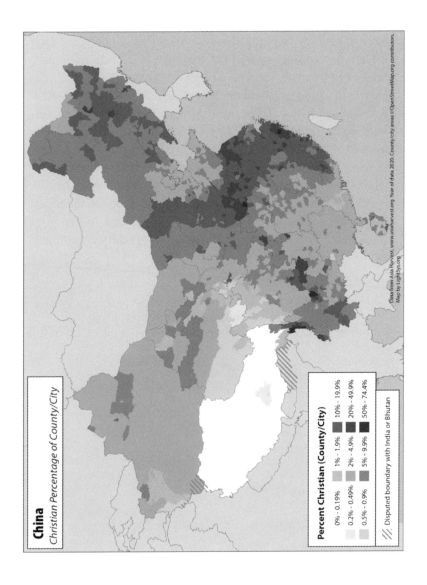

China
Christian Percentage of County/City

Percent Christian (County/City)

0% - 0.19%   1% - 1.9%   10% - 19.9%
0.2% - 0.49%   2% - 4.9%   20% - 49.9%
0.5% - 0.9%   5% - 9.9%   50% - 74.4%

/// Disputed boundary with India or Bhutan

Data from Asia Harvest. www.asiaharvest.org. Year of data 2020. County/city areas ©OpenStreetMap.org contributors.
Map by LightSys.org

Notes

The China Chronicles Overview

1   R. Wardlaw Thompson, *Griffith John: The Story of Fifty Years in China* (London: Religious Tract Society, 1908), p. 65.

Introduction

1   F. P. Gilman, M. M. M. and J. W. Lowrie, *The Isle of Palms: Sketches of Hainan, The American Presbyterian Mission Island of Hainan, South China* (Shanghai: Commercial Press, 1919), p. 1.

2   Leonard Clark, "Among the Big Knot Lois of Hainan," *National Geographic* (September 1938), p. 391.

3   Gilman and Lowrie, *The Isle of Palms*, p. 8.

4   Clark, "Among the Big Knot Lois of Hainan," p. 410.

5   William J. Leverett, "A Babel of Tongues in Hainan," *The Missionary Review of the World* (December 1900), p. 940.

6   Leverett, "A Babel of Tongues in Hainan," p. 940.

7   Margaret Moninger, "Field News: Sama, Hainan," *Friends of Moslems* (January 1943), p. 15.

8   Eduardo Baptista, "Tiny Muslim Community in China's Hainan becomes Latest Target for Religious Crackdown," *South China Morning Post* (September 28, 2020).

9   Michael Buckley et.al., *China: A Travel Survival Kit* (Hawthorn, Australia: Lonely Planet Publications), 1994, pp. 289–90.

10   Personal communication, April 2022.

11   Antoinette Radford, "US Sources Insist Chinese Balloon was Military," BBC News (February 8, 2023).

Catholics in Hainan

1   Gilman and Lowrie, *The Isle of Palms*, pp. 47–48.

2   Gilman and Lowrie, *The Isle of Palms*, p. 48.

3   Gilman and Lowrie, *The Isle of Palms*, pp. 48–49.

4   B. C. Henry, "Glimpses of Hainan," *Chinese Recorder and Missionary Journal* (May–June 1883), pp. 168–69.

5 *The Catholic Encyclopedia, Volume VIII* (New York: Robert Appleton Co., 1910).

6 Compiled from diocese statistics at www.catholic-hierarchy.org .

7 "New Church Organizations Set Up on Hainan," *Bridge* (January–February 1988), p. 19.

Carl Jeremiassen

1 Karl Gützlaff, *Journal of Three Voyages Along the Coast of China in 1831, 1832 and 1833* (London: Frederick Westley and A. H. Davies, 1834), p. 83.

2 Not only is Jeremiassen an obscure family name in Denmark, but an extensive search of the Danish maritime archives failed to turn up a nineteenth-century sea captain or sailor by that name. Today, the family name Jeremiassen is more commonly found in Greenland.

3 Gilman and Lowrie, *The Isle of Palms*, p. 106.

4 Gilman and Lowrie, *The Isle of Palms*, p. 51.

5 H. M. McCandliss, "Medical Experiences During Forty Years in China," *The China Medical Journal* (October 1925), pp. 934–35.

6 G. Thompson Brown, *Earthen Vessels and Transcendent Power: American Presbyterians in China, 1837–1952* (Maryknoll, NY: Orbis Books, 1997), pp. 90–92. It may be that Jeremiassen first visited Hainan in 1869 but returned to the mainland and did not fully reside on the island until 1881.

7 Brown, *Earthen Vessels and Transcendent Power*, p. 90.

8 Brown, *Earthen Vessels and Transcendent Power*, p. 91.

9 *Chinese Recorder and Missionary Journal* (December 1882), p. 469.

10 Henry, "Glimpses of Hainan," pp. 168–69.

11 Henry, "Glimpses of Hainan," pp. 305–6.

12 *Chinese Recorder and Missionary Journal* (July 1885), p. 280.

13 *The Christian Alliance and Foreign Missionary Weekly* (June 8, 1894), p. 636.

14 *Chinese Recorder and Missionary Journal* (July 1886), p. 275.

15 Frank P. Gilman, "Hainan and its Missionary Work," *Chinese Recorder and Missionary Journal* (June 1890), p. 278.

16 Gilman, "Hainan and its Missionary Work," p. 275.

17 Brown, *Earthen Vessels and Transcendent Power*, p. 92.

18 Marshall Broomhall (ed.), *The Chinese Empire: A General and Missionary Survey* (London: Morgan & Scott, 1907), pp. 409–10.

19 Frank P. Gilman, "In Memoriam," *Chinese Recorder and Missionary Journal* (August 1901), p. 412.

20 Clark, "Among the Big Knot Lois of Hainan," p. 418.

Henry McCandliss

1 *The Christian Alliance* (February 1888), p. 32.
2 Brown, *Earthen Vessels and Transcendent Power*, p. 92.
3 McCandliss, "Medical Experiences During Forty Years in China," p. 935.
4 McCandliss, "Medical Experiences During Forty Years in China," p. 936.
5 McCandliss, "Medical Experiences During Forty Years in China," pp. 943–44.
6 Cited in Margaret Moninger, *Hainan Newsletter* (Summer 1926), p. 10.

1890s

1 *The Missionary Review of the World* (May 1893), pp. 397–98.
2 Dr. A. W. Douthwaite, "Relation of the Marriage Question to Missionary Work," an address delivered in London in 1898, cited in Linda K. Benson, *Across China's Gobi: The Lives of Evangeline French, Mildred Cable, and Francesca French of the China Inland Mission* (Manchester, UK: Eastbridge Books, 2008), p. 10.
3 John R. Mott, cited in Hannah Davies, *Among Hills and Valleys in Western China: Incidents of Missionary Work* (London: S. W. Patridge & Co., 1901), p. 44.
4 *The Christian and Missionary Alliance* (May 18, 1898), p. 474.
5 *The Christian and Missionary Alliance* (September 28, 1898), p. 306.
6 Gilman and Lowrie, *The Isle of Palms*, p. 56.
7 *The Christian and Missionary Alliance* (July 29, 1899), p. 142.

1900s and 1910s

1 Brown, *Earthen Vessels and Transcendent Power*, p. 199.
2 Henry H. Bucher, "Experiences of a Missionary in Hainan," *The Missionary Review of the World* (May 1939), p. 247.
3 *Chinese Recorder and Missionary Journal* (November 1902), pp. 579–80.
4 Brown, *Earthen Vessels and Transcendent Power*, p. 199.
5 Brown, *Earthen Vessels and Transcendent Power*, p. 199.
6 Gilman and Lowrie, *The Isle of Palms*, pp. 24–25.
7 Gilman and Lowrie, *The Isle of Palms*, p. 52.
8 *The Missionary Review of the World* (April 1914), p. 307.
9 *The Catholic Encyclopedia*, Vol. VIII.
10 *The Missionary Review of the World* (October 1915), pp. 787–88.
11 *The Missionary Review of the World* (February 1916), p. 142.
12 Gilman and Lowrie, *The Isle of Palms*, pp. 55, 57.
13 Gilman, "Hainan and its Missionary Work," p. 280.

14 *Chinese Recorder and Missionary Journal* (January 1900), p. 33.
15 *Chinese Recorder and Missionary Journal* (January 1918), pp. 52–53.
16 Gilman and Lowrie, *The Isle of Palms*, pp. 109–10.
17 From Gilman and Lowrie, *The Isle of Palms*, Appendix D.

1920s

1 Gilman and Lowrie, *The Isle of Palms*, p. 56.
2 *The Missionary Review of the World* (January 1925), p. 72.
3 Nathaniel Bercovitz, "The Present Value of Medical Missions," *The Missionary Review of the World* (December 1934), p. 562.
4 Bercovitz, "The Present Value of Medical Missions," pp. 562–63.
5 Bercovitz, "The Present Value of Medical Missions," p. 563.
6 David S. Tappan, "A Missionary Hero of Hainan," *The Missionary Review of the World* (October 1924), p. 816.
7 Kathleen L. Lodwick, *The Widow's Quest: The Byers Extraterritorial Case in Hainan, China, 1924–1925* (Studies in Christianity in China) (Bethlehem, PA: Lehigh University Press, 2003), p. 60.
8 Lodwick, *The Widow's Quest*, p. 30.
9 *The Missionary Review of the World* (September 1924), p. 744.
10 *Chinese Recorder and Missionary Journal* (August 1924), p. 531.
11 Tappan, "A Missionary Hero of Hainan," p. 816.
12 *The Missionary Review of the World* (October 1924), p. 836.
13 Lodwick, *The Widow's Quest*, p. 32.
14 *The Pentecostal Holiness Advocate* (June 10, 1926), p. 14.
15 From Milton T. Stauffer, *The Christian Occupation of China* (Shanghai: China Continuation Committee, 1922), p. xxv.
16 Brown, *Earthen Vessels and Transcendent Power*, p. 202.
17 Arthur Rugh, "What the Chinese Think of Christianity," *The Missionary Review of the World* (March 1926), p. 202.

1930s

1 *Hainan Newsletter* (Autumn 1933), p. 1.
2 *The Missionary Review of the World* (August 1931), p. 627.
3 *The Missionary Review of the World* (July 1936), p. 360.
4 "Table 3: People Groups in Hainan" in the appendix of this book.
5 Bucher, "Experiences of a Missionary in Hainan," p. 246.
6 From the Henry Hale Bucher, Sr. and Louise Scott Bucher Papers at the Yale University Archives.
7 Brown, *Earthen Vessels and Transcendent Power*, p. 202.

8 *The Missionary Review of the World* (March 1932), p. 185.

9 *Bridge: Church Life in China Today* (January–February 1988).

The Kim Mun

1 Kathleen L. Lodwick, *Educating the Women of Hainan: The Career of Margaret Moninger in China 1915–1942* (Lexington, KY: University Press of Kentucky, 1995), p. 77.

2 Clark, "Among the Big Knot Lois of Hainan," pp. 415–16.

3 Paul Hattaway, *Operation China: Introducing all the Peoples of China* (Carlisle, UK: Piquant Books, 2000), p. 252.

4 Brown, *Earthen Vessels and Transcendent Power*, p. 200.

5 Lodwick, *Educating the Women of Hainan*, p. 76.

6 Gilman and Lowrie, *The Isle of Palms*, pp. 83–84. Margaret Moninger is listed as one of two editors of the book, using her initials M. M. M.

7 *The Missionary Review of the World* (February 1919), p. 118.

8 Lodwick, *Educating the Women of Hainan*, p. 80.

9 "The Miao People of Nanmao Encounter Christianity," *Bridge* (January–February 1988), p. 9.

10 "The Miao People of Nanmao Encounter Christianity," p. 9.

11 *The Missionary Review of the World* (May 1927), p. 382.

12 *The Missionary Review of the World* (December 1937), p. 609.

13 *Tianfeng* (June 2006).

14 *Tianfeng* (July 1985), cited in *Pray for China* (May 1986), p. 10.

15 "The Miao People of Nanmao Encounter Christianity," p. 9.

1940s and 1950s

1 *The Alliance Weekly* (November 25, 1939), p. 752.

2 Lodwick, *Educating the Women of Hainan*, p. 24.

3 Lodwick, *Educating the Women of Hainan*, p. 147.

4 Lodwick, *Educating the Women of Hainan*, p. 44.

5 Lodwick, *Educating the Women of Hainan*, p. 76.

6 Lodwick, *Educating the Women of Hainan*, p. 76.

7 Lodwick, *Educating the Women of Hainan*, p. 77.

8 Kathleen L. Lodwick, *How Christianity Came to China: A Brief History* (Minneapolis, MN: Fortress Press. 1916), Kindle edition.

9 Lodwick, *Educating the Women of Hainan*, p. 207.

10 Lodwick, *Educating the Women of Hainan*, back cover.

11 China Inland Mission, *The Obstinate Horse and Other Stories* (London: China Inland Mission, 1955), p. 37.

12 China Inland Mission, *The Obstinate Horse*, pp. 44–46.

1960s and 1970s

1 Paul E. Kauffman, *Through China's Open Door* (Hong Kong: Asian Outreach, 1979), p. 128.
2 "Signs and Wonders in Communist China," *Asian Report* (June 1982).
3 "The Price of Christian Leadership," *Asian Report* (Vol. 14, No. 3), p. 4.
4 "The Price of Christian Leadership," *Asian Report*, p. 5.
5 "The Price of Christian Leadership," *Asian Report*, p. 5.
6 "The Price of Christian Leadership," *Asian Report*, p. 6.
7 Jonathan Chao, *Wise as Serpents, Harmless as Doves* (Pasadena, CA: William Carey Library, 1988), p. 116.
8 TSPM China Prayer Calendar, 2002.
9 Tony Lambert, *China's Christian Millions: The Costly Revival* (London: Monarch, 1999), p. 215.
10 "Table 2: All Christians in Hainan" in the appendix of this book.
11 Marjorie Baker, *Where Angels Tread* (Hong Kong: Asian Outreach, c. 1982), pp. 23–24.
12 Baker, *Where Angels Tread*, pp. 25–26.
13 Baker, *Where Angels Tread*, p. 26.

The Indonesians

1 "The Gereja Batania," *Bridge* (January–February 1990), pp. 16–17.
2 Letter from Hainan, 1961, in Leslie T. Lyall, *Red Sky at Night: Communism Confronts Christianity in China* (London: Hodder and Stoughton, 1969), p. 118.
3 Lyall, *Red Sky at Night*, p. 118.
4 Lyall, *Red Sky at Night*, p. 119.
5 Letter to Far East Broadcasting, February 1987.
6 *The Alliance Weekly* (February 17, 1954), p. 7.
7 "The Gereja Batania," *Bridge*, pp. 16–17.
8 "The Gereja Batania," *Bridge*, pp. 16–17.

1980s

1 "Signs and Wonders in Communist China," *Asian Report* (June 1982).
2 Leslie T. Lyall, *God Reigns in China* (London: Hodder & Stoughton, 1985), p. 170.
3 "Signs and Wonders in Communist China," *Asian Report* (June 1982).
4 Letter to Asian Outreach in *Asian Report* (September–October 1985), p. 17.

5 "A Tale of Two Timothies," *Asian Report* (March–April 1988), pp. 20–23.

6 Jonathan Chao (ed.), *The China Mission Handbook: A Portrait of China and its Church* (Hong Kong: Chinese Church Research Center, 1989), p. 108.

7 *Tianfeng* (July 1985), cited in *Pray for China* (May 1986), p. 10.

8 Julia and Kevin Garratt, *Two Tears on the Window: Shadows of Prison, Reflections of Hope* (Victoria, Canada: First Choice Books, 2018), p. 25.

9 Garratt, *Two Tears on the Window*, p. 27.

1990s

1 "Anecdotes from My First Term," an unpublished report by a Hainan missionary.

2 "Gereja Kemah Peremuan—Second Indonesian Church in Hainan," *Bridge* (May 1992), p. 15.

3 *Bridge* (January–February 1988).

4 Personal communication, January 2023.

5 *The Hainan Herald* (Summer 1993).

6 "Video 01, Importance of Multiplication" from a YouTube series of messages by Curtis Sergeant entitled *Multiplication Concepts*. https://www.youtube.com/watch?v=IAfRti1Wyqs&list=PLtMNe_ry3iGBIE4fqiCyoZIu7-XU_gLh8&index=2.

7 "Endvisioning: A Case Study in Reverse Problem-Solving," an unpublished missionary report by a Hainan missionary.

8 "Anecdotes from My First Term."

9 "Anecdotes from My First Term."

10 "Endvisioning: A Case Study in Reverse Problem-Solving."

11 Personal report from Training Evangelistic Leadership, August 1992.

12 *Pray for China* (May–June 1992).

13 *Pray for China* (January–February 1996).

14 Far East Broadcasting, July 1996.

15 Far East Broadcasting, August 1997.

16 Far East Broadcasting, April 1999.

17 Far East Broadcasting, July 1999.

When Heaven Came to Hainan

1 "Video 11A, Prayer Walking Evangelism Story," from a YouTube series of messages by Curtis Sergeant entitled *Multiplication Concepts*. https://www.youtube.com/watch?v=JH80rBz3tuk&list=PLtMNe_ry3iGBIE4fqiCyoZIu7-XU_gLh8&index=13.

2 J. Edwin Orr, *The Re-Study of Revival and Revivalism* (Pasadena, CA: School of World Mission, 1981), pp. i–ii.

3 https://en.wikipedia.org/wiki/1904%E2%80%931905_Welsh_revival.

4 https://www.pbs.org/wgbh/pages/frontline/godinamerica/people/charles-finney.html.

5 "Anecdotes from My First Term."

Stories from the Frontlines

1 "Anecdotes from My First Term."

2 "Hainan Province: China's Forgotten Corner," *Pray for China* (January–February 1996), p. 128.

3 Newsletter by an American missionary who wishes to remain anonymous.

4 *The Hainan Herald* (Summer 1993).

5 Newsletter by an American missionary.

6 Carl Lawrence with David Wang, *The Coming Influence of China* (Sisters, OR: Multnomah Publishers, 1996), pp. 186–92.

7 Lawrence with Wang, *The Coming Influence of China*, p. 189.

8 Lawrence with Wang, *The Coming Influence of China*, p. 191.

9 Lawrence with Wang, *The Coming Influence of China*, p. 191.

10 "Anecdotes from My First Term."

11 "Video 15, What About Heresy," from a YouTube series of messages by Curtis Sergeant entitled *Multiplication Concepts*. https://www.youtube.com/watch?v=8hlFt6lY3_U&list=PLtMNe_ry3iGBIE4fqiCyoZIu7-XU_gLh8&index=17. This concept of small group church structures proving to be more solid platforms for propagating biblical doctrine was also discussed in Frank Viola and George Barna, *Pagan Christianity: Exploring the Roots of Our Church Practices* (Carol Stream, IL: Tyndale Momentum, 2012).

12 Personal interview with the missionary, October 1998.

13 Personal interview with the missionary, October 1998.

14 "Anecdotes from My First Term."

15 Personal communication, January 2023.

The Li

1 Chungshee Halen Lui, "Hai-nan-tao Li-ren wen-shen chih ven chiu" ["A study of Tattoo of the Li of Hainan Island"], *Bulletin of Ethnological Studies* (Vol. 1, 1936), p. 201.

2 "The Li People," *On Target* (June 2003).

3 William J. Leverett, "A Babel of Tongues in Hainan," *The Missionary Review of the World* (December 1900), p. 941.

4 Clark, "Among the Big Knot Lois of Hainan," p. 408.

5 Clark, "Among the Big Knot Lois of Hainan," pp. 410–11.

6 Lars Krutak, "At the Tail of the Dragon: Vanishing Tattoos of China's Li People," https://www.larskrutak.com/at-the-tail-of-the-dragon-the-vanishing-tattoos-of-chinas-li-people/.

7 Clark, "Among the Big Knot Lois of Hainan," p. 410.

8 Gilman and Lowrie, *The Isle of Palms*, p. 15.

9 Krutak, "At the Tail of the Dragon."

10 Brown, *Earthen Vessels and Transcendent Power*, p. 199.

11 Gilman and Lowrie, *The Isle of Palms*, pp. 72–73.

12 *The Missionary Review of the World* (September 1936), p. 441.

13 Bucher, "Experiences of a Missionary in Hainan," p. 248.

14 Leung Sze Tai, "Christmas at the Foot of Five-Finger Mountain," *Bridge* (January–February 1988), pp. 5–6.

15 Tai, "Christmas at the Foot of Five-Finger Mountain," p. 8.

16 Tai, "Christmas at the Foot of Five-Finger Mountain," p. 8.

17 "The Lamp on the Southernmost Tip of China," *Tianfeng* (September 1990), translated in *China Study Journal* (November 1991), p. 63.

18 Su Shan, "How Can We Stop?" *Asian Report* (May–June 1992), p. 22.

19 "The Li People," *On Target* (June 2003).

20 "The Li People," *On Target* (June 2003).

21 "Hainan Island: Part 2—The House Church Revival," *Asia Harvest* (November 2004), pp. 6–8.

22 "Hainan Island: Part 2," *Asia Harvest* (November 2004), pp. 6–8.

2000s

1 "Anecdotes from My First Term."

2 "Hainan Province: China's Forgotten Corner," *Pray for China*, p. 128.

3 Personal communication with a Hainan missionary, March 2007.

4 *AsiaLink* (Summer 2006), pp. 1–3.

5 Patrick Johnstone and Jason Mandryk, *Operation World: 21st Century Edition* (Carlisle, UK: Paternoster Lifestyle, 2001), p. 171.

6 Lambert, *China's Christian Millions*, pp. 214–15.

7 The official figure of 37,000 Evangelical believers in Hainan was first published by Three-Self sources in the early 1990s and was subsequently repeated by many publications, including *Bridge* (May 1992).

8 Personal communication with a Hainan missionary, April 2002.

9 Personal communication with a Hainan missionary, April 2002.

10 Personal communication with a Hainan missionary, April 2002.

11 Personal communication, September 2003.

12 OMF International, "Survey of the Chinese Church: Part II," *Global Chinese Ministries* (April 2003).

13 Johnstone and Mandryk, *Operation World: 21st Century Edition*, p. 171.

14 Jason Mandryk, *Operation World: The Definitive Prayer Guide to Every Nation* (Colorado Springs: Biblica, 2010), p. 234.

15 *Pray for China* (February–March 2001).

16 *Lift up Our Holy Hands* (July 2001).

17 Far East Broadcasting, November 2001.

18 *Lift up Our Holy Hands* (June 2002).

19 *Pray for China* (June–July 2003).

20 Far East Broadcasting, April 2004.

21 Letter to CCI, October 2004.

22 Letter to CCI, February 2005.

23 Letter to CCI, June 2006.

2010s and 2020s

1 "Hainan Christians Violently Beaten for Preventing Construction on Building Site of Christian Church after Government Illicitly Sold Site to Developers," *China Aid* (August 13, 2013).

2 "Government Shuts Down At Least a Dozen House Churches in Hainan Province," *China Aid* (June 1, 2013).

3 "Table 2: All Christians in Hainan" in the appendix of this book. Mandryk, *Operation World* (2010), p. 234, listed a percentage which amounts to 112,000 TSPM believers in Hainan. The overall official TSPM figure for Hainan remains low, even though their own statistics by county add up to much greater than their provincial total.

4 Personal communication with someone who attended the meeting, November 2016.

The Future of the Church in Hainan

1 Mimi Lau, "China Doubles Down Against Foreign Teachers Spreading Christianity," *South China Morning Post* (September 6, 2020).

Researching Christians in China

1 Ye's figure was quoted in numerous publications at the time, including the *2007 Annual Report of the Congressional-Executive Commission on China: One Hundred Tenth Congress*, First Session (October 10, 2007).

2 Ku Ma, "Rule of Law Best Help to Freedom of Faith," *China Daily* (December 3, 2009).

Selected Bibliography

American Presbyterian Mission, *Annual Report of the American Presbyterian Mission, Hainan, for the Year Ending November 1, 1906* (Shanghai: American Presbyterian Mission Press, 1907).

Broomhall, Marshall (ed.), *The Chinese Empire: A General and Missionary Survey* (London: Morgan & Scott, 1907).

Brown, G. Thompson, *Earthen Vessels and Transcendent Power: American Presbyterians in China, 1837–1952* (Maryknoll, NY: Orbis Books, 1997).

Chao, Jonathan, *Wise as Serpents, Harmless as Doves* (Pasadena, CA: William Carey Library, 1988).

Covell, Ralph R., *The Liberating Gospel in China: The Christian Faith Among China's Minority Peoples* (Grand Rapids, MI: Baker Book House Company, 1995).

Crisler, Clarence C., *China's Borderlands and Beyond* (Takoma Park, MD: Review and Herald Publishing Association, 1937).

Dodd, William Clifton, *The Tai Race: Elder Brother of the Chinese* (Cedar Rapids, IA: The Torch Press, 1923).

Estep, William R., *Whole Gospel Whole World: The Foreign Mission Board of the Southern Baptist Convention 1845–1995* (Nashville, TN: Broadman & Holman, 1994).

Fulton, Mary H., *Inasmuch: Extracts from Letters, Journals, Papers, etc.* (West Medford, MA: Central Committee on the United Study of Foreign Missions, 1915).

Fung, Raymond, *Households of God on China's Soil* (Maryknoll, NY: Orbis, 1982).

Garratt, Julie and Kevin, *Two Tears on the Window: Shadows of Prison, Reflections of Hope* (Victoria, Canada: First Choice Books, 2018).

Gih, Andrew, *Launch out into the Deep* (London: Marshall, Morgan & Scott, 1938).

Gilman, F. P., M. M. M. and J. W. Lowrie, *The Isle of Palms: Sketches of Hainan, The American Presbyterian Mission Island of Hainan, South China* (Shanghai: Commercial Press, 1919).

Hattaway, Paul, *Operation China: Introducing all the Peoples of China* (Carlisle, UK: Piquant Books, 2000).

Henry, B. C., *Ling-nam, or Interior Views of Southern China: Including*

Explorations in the Hitherto Untraversed Island of Hainan (London: S. W. Patridge & Co., 1886).

Henry, Benjamin C., *The Cross and the Dragon, or, Light in the Broad East* (Classic Reprint) (London: Forgotten Books, 2018).

Kauffman, Paul E., *Through China's Open Door* (Hong Kong: Asian Outreach, 1979).

Lambert, Tony, *China's Christian Millions* (Oxford: Monarch, 2006).

Latourette, Kenneth Scott, *A History of Christian Missions in China* (New York: Macmillan & Co, 1929).

Lawrence, Carl, with David Wang, *The Coming Influence of China* (Sisters, OR: Multnomah Publishers, 1996).

Lodwick, Kathleen L., *Educating the Women of Hainan: The Career of Margaret Moninger in China 1915–1942* (Lexington, KY: University Press of Kentucky, 1995).

_____, *How Christianity Came to China: A Brief History* (Minneapolis, MN: Fortress Press, 1916).

_____, *The Widow's Quest: The Byers Extraterritorial Case in Hainan, China, 1924–1925* (Studies in Christianity in China) (Bethlehem, PA: Lehigh University Press, 2003).

Lyall, Leslie T., *God Reigns in China* (London: Hodder & Stoughton, 1985).

_____, *Red Sky at Night: Communism Confronts Christianity in China* (London: Hodder and Stoughton, 1969).

MacDonald, Margaret, *Roderick MacDonald, MD: A Servant of Jesus Christ* (London: Robert Culley, 1908).

MacGillivray, D. (ed.), *A Century of Protestant Missions in China, 1807–1907* (Shanghai: American Presbyterian Mission Press, 1907).

Maryknoll Mission, Maryknoll Mission Letters (New York: Macmillan & Co, 1923).

Ma Yin (ed.), *China's Minority Nationalities* (Beijing: Foreign Languages Press, 1989).

Moser, Leo J., *The Chinese Mosaic: The Peoples and Provinces of China* (Boulder, CO: Westview Press, 1985).

Murray, Jeremy A., *China's Lonely Revolution: The Local Communist Movement of Hainan Island, 1926–1956* (Albany, NY: State University of New York Press, 2017).

Newton, C. H., *Hainan: The Land South of the Sea* (New York: Board of Foreign Missions of the Presbyterian Church in the USA, no date).

Ramsey, S. Robert, *The Languages of China* (Princeton, NJ: Princeton University Press, 1987).

Selected Bibliography

Schaeffer, K. L., *Hainan's Daughters* (Chicago: Women's Presbyterian Board of Missions of the Northwest, no date).

Schafer, Edward H., *Shore of Pearls* (Berkeley, CA: University of California Press, 1970).

Stauffer, Milton T. (ed.), *The Christian Occupation of China* (Shanghai: China Continuation Committee, 1922).

Tamabima, Hadul (ed.), *The Voice of the Minorities: The Beautiful Feet of the Messengers of the Gospel Among Ethnic Minorities* (Paradise, PA: Ambassadors for Christ, 2007).

Contact Details

———•◦•———

Paul Hattaway is the founder and director of Asia Harvest, a non-denominational ministry which serves the church in Asia through various strategic initiatives, including Bible printing and supporting Asian missionaries sharing the gospel among unreached peoples.

The author can be reached by email at **office@asiaharvest.org**, or by writing to him via any of the addresses listed below.

For more than thirty years Asia Harvest has served the church in Asia through strategic projects that equip the local churches. At the time of print, Asia Harvest has successfully printed and delivered more than 420,000 Bibles to house church Christians in Hainan, in addition to supporting many evangelists and providing aid to hundreds of persecuted church leaders and their families.

Opportunities exist for interested Christians to support native evangelists working among many of China's minority groups through the Asian Workers' Fund.

If you would like to receive the free *Asia Harvest* newsletter, order other volumes in The China Chronicles series or Paul's other books, or if you want to contribute to Paul's ministries to support Chinese Christian workers and their families, please visit **www.asiaharvest.org** or write to the address below nearest you:

Asia Harvest USA & Canada
353 Jonestown Rd #320
Winston-Salem, NC 27104
USA

Asia Harvest Australia
Mailbox 80, 377 Kent Street
Seabridge House
Sydney, NSW 2000
AUSTRALIA

Asia Harvest New Zealand
PO Box 1757
Queenstown, 9348
NEW ZEALAND

Asia Harvest UK
c/o AsiaLink
31A Main Street
Ballyclare
Co. Antrim BT39 9AA
UNITED KINGDOM

Asia Harvest Europe
c/o Stiftung SALZ
Moehringer Landstr. 98
70563 Stuttgart
GERMANY